177 St Parkchester
Westchester Av
St Lawrence Av
Westchester Av
Morrison Av
Soundview Av
Westchester Av
Elder Av
Westchester Av
Whitlock Av
Westchester Av
Hunts Point Av
So Blvd
Longwood Av
So Blvd
E 149 St
So Blvd
Roosevelt Av
Jackson Hgts
Northern Blvd
Bway
65 St
Bway
74 St
Bway
Steinway St
Bway
46 St
Bway
69 St Fisk Av
Roosevelt Av
36 St
Northern Blvd
61 St-Woodside
Roosevelt Av LIRR
33 St
Rawson St
Queens Blvd
40 St
Lowery St
Queens Blvd
Queens
Plaza
Queens
IND
Van Alst-21 St
Jackson Av
Greenpoint Av
Manhattan Av
I0605071

ARMIES
OF THE
NIGHT

THE WARRIORS AND ITS LEGACY

MICHAEL GINGOLD &
CHRIS POGGIALI

ARMIES OF THE NIGHT:
THE WARRIORS AND ITS LEGACY

This is a work of nonfiction. The events and experiences detailed herein have been faithfully rendered as remembered by the author and interviewees, to the best of their ability. Except where noted, quotations were obtained directly by the authors.

COVER DESIGN: Hag Cult
LAYOUT: Arkadii Pankevich

Image credits appear in the back of the book.

LIBRARY OF CONGRESS CONTROL NUMBER: 2025942133
LC record available at https://lccn.loc.gov/2025942133

ISBNs: 9781948221979 (hardcover), 9781948221962 (ebook)

Printed in USA.

1984 PUBLISHING
Cleveland, Ohio / USA
1984Publishing.com
info@1984publishing.com

FIRST EDITION / FIRST PRINTING

For everyone, alive or deceased, who worked in front of and/or behind the camera on this cult film favorite.

– Chris and Michael

Contents

Introduction

On February 15, 1979, a 16-year-old high-school sophomore named Martin Yakubowicz was waiting for a Boston subway when he ran into a group of similarly aged acquaintances. They decided to ride home together, but after they departed the train at the Fields Corner Station in the Dorchester neighborhood, one of that group, Michael Barrett, began drunkenly challenging Yakubowicz, and wound up stabbing him with a knife. Yakubowicz died six hours later.

Barrett was eventually sentenced to 12 to 15 years in jail, but the details of his trial and punishment for his crime are not immediately evident when one does an on-line search for stories about the incident. What does come up first, and what made the murder particularly newsworthy at the time, had to do with where Barrett and his friends had gone before they even boarded the subway. They had been at Boston's Saxon Theatre attending Paramount Pictures' *The Warriors*, a film that the press was already holding at least partially responsible for the deaths of two other teenagers in California. Yakubowicz's murder fanned the flames already burning under *The Warriors*, which became a lightning rod for the criticism and debate about reel vs. real violence that had been ongoing through much of the 1970s.

As with many movies that became notorious for their brutality in that decade and the early 1980s, including horror films such as *The Texas Chain Saw Massacre* (1974) and even *Friday the 13th* (1980, also released by Paramount), *The Warriors* can seem rather tame today, especially when compared to the cinematic output of the last couple of decades. Although its premise is predicated on violent conflict, *The Warriors* contains little actual blood, and director Walter Hill's approach is stylized "almost to the point of being sci-fi...filled with some fantasy images," as the director told the *New York Post*'s Stephen M. Silverman during its production in 1978.

Watching it now (and to be fair, a few critics at the time pointed this out, as we'll see), *The Warriors* hardly seems like the type of picture to rile an audience to the point of inspiring real-life attacks, or to become a *bête noire* for those seeking to alert and protect the public from the insidious influences of a sensationalistic Hollywood.

The controversy around it may have faded, but *The Warriors* remains a singular and influential achievement in action cinema, whose echoes are still sounding in movies today. Like its contemporaries *Star Wars* (1977) and *Halloween* (1978), it scored as a popular box-office success upon first release while also becoming a cult film in the subsequent years. As time passed, both that notoriety and the initially negative critical response faded away, and *The Warriors* built a following via its exposure on various video formats and retrospective screenings. Today it is regarded as one of the touchstone films of its decade, one that has been spun off into comic books, action figures, video and board games and a concept album (and potential stage musical) by one of the most celebrated writers/lyricists of our time. The picture that had once been reviled by the mainstream has now been fully embraced by it.

First conceived by author Sol Yurick in his 1965 novel as an urban variation on the Greek epic *Anabasis*, initially intended for screen translation by the drive-in specialists at American International Pictures, and hustled quickly into production when another project by Hill and producer Lawrence Gordon fell through, *The Warriors* underwent a journey as eventful as that undertaken by its central characters. The titular street gang's quest to make their way home to Coney Island, losing members and fighting rivals along the way, only to find their greatest trouble awaiting them once they've made it home, is reflected in the saga of the movie itself.

1 *The Warriors*: Literary Origins and Early Incarnations

"I think the elements for *The Warriors* began to come together sometime during the '50s," wrote author Sol Yurick in the introduction to the 2003 edition of his most famous work. "I was having a talk with a friend of mine, a writer whose mother and father had been successful Hollywood script writers. He was trying to explain to me what constituted a good idea (the 'high concept') for a script. Almost as a joke, I hit upon the notion of a story of a fighting gang based on, or paralleling, the course of *The Anabasis*. Once uttered, I dropped the idea. I thought the notion was ingenious, but not really serious. Yet I didn't forget it."

Yurick's first exposure to Xenophon's *Anabasis* had come during his undergraduate studies at New York University, which he attended on the G.I. Bill after a prolonged illness brought him a medical discharge from the U.S. Army in 1945. A graduate of the Bronx High School of Science, Yurick had trained as a surgical technician in the military and was interested in becoming a scientist but really had no aptitude for mathematics. Instead, he majored in literature with a philosophy minor, and it was during these years at NYU that he decided to become a writer. Although Yurick considered his literary heroes to be Kafka, Dostoyevsky, Joyce and Proust, it was *Anabasis*—which was never an assigned text in any of his courses—that was the inspiration for his first published novel.

Composed by Xenophon around 370 B.C., *Anabasis* exists in numerous translations and under several titles including *The March of the Ten Thousand*, *The March Up Country*, *The Anabasis of Xenophon* and *The*

Anabasis of Cyrus. The edition Yurick read in college was the Rex Warner translation, published in 1949 by Penguin as *The Persian Expedition*.

For those unfamiliar with the book under any title, here is the story in fewer than 500 words...

Penguin's hardcover edition of *The Persian Expedition* (c. 1949), translated by Rex Warner.

King Darius II of Persia dies in 404 B.C. and leaves the throne to his elder son, Artaxerxes II. Darius' other son, Cyrus the Younger, is imprisoned for plotting to usurp the throne from his brother until Parysatis, their mother, convinces Artaxerxes to free him. Cyrus enlists a Spartan exile named Clearchus and his Hellenic mercenaries to accompany him on a march into the capitol city of Babylon to overthrow Artaxerxes. Along the way, they plunder Tarsus, burn the palace in Syria, cross the Euphrates and march through Arabia. Upon arrival in Babylon, the army amounts to 12,900 Hellenes and 100,000 nationals, but there are over one million Persians waiting for them. Most of Cyrus' army is in disorder, yet he still takes on Artaxerxes at the Battle of Cunaxa. The larger Persian forces flee the area, but not before Cyrus is killed.

The next day, Artaxerxes sends messengers who tell the Hellenes that he is the victor because Cyrus is dead and the Persians have won the battle. He insists they lay down their arms, but the Hellenes refuse and a truce is called. The Hellenes are told to stay where they are and the truce will hold, but if they march forward or back, it will mean war. Clearchus will only agree to the truce if Artaxerxes provides breakfast for the troops. A compromise is reached: The remaining Hellenes will march peacefully home with an escort. Days pass with no sign of the escort, and Clearchus believes Artaxerxes is stalling so he can organize his forces to block the path back to Hellas. Tissaphernes finally shows up with troops to escort Clearchus and the Hellenes back to the Black Sea. However, neither the Hellenes nor the Persian escort troops trust each other, so Clearchus—accompanied by five officers and 20 soldiers—agrees to meet with Tissaphernes to settle the misunderstanding. It turns out to be a trap, and Clearchus and his men are executed before the royal court in Babylon.

Artaxerxes again demands that the Hellenes lay down their arms. An Athenian writer named Xenophon joins the remaining officers and gives his advice. He is chosen as one of the five new captains, and they begin their march to the sea. In addition to fighting Persians, they encounter Carduchoi (Kurds), Armenians, Chaldeans, Taochians, Chalybeans, Scythians, Colchians, Trapezuntines, Mossynoecians, Paphlagonians, Drillae and others, on a march through mountains and deserts, snow and heat, until the 10,000 finally reach "The sea! The sea!"

Ten years after graduating from NYU, Yurick was back in school, this time at Brooklyn College earning an M.A. in English and planning to become a teacher. During this period, he also saw his first short story appear in print when "The Annealing" was included in the second issue of Saul Bellow's short-lived literary journal *The Noble Savage*. "Publication hardened my resolve to be a full-time writer rather than a teacher. I was given permission to write a novel as my master's thesis. This became *Fertig*, which played a critical role in my development as a writer and, indirectly, in the formation of *The Warriors*."

It took more than a year for Yurick to write *Fertig*, and longer for it to find a publisher. As more and more rejections slips came in, Yurick fought despair by starting work on the high-concept story he had come up with back in the mid-'50s: the 10,000 as a New York street gang. During his years between college and graduate school, he had worked as an investigator with the New York City Department of Welfare and therefore had first-hand experience to draw from, but still needed to do a great deal of research. This included everything from interviewing gang members and youth officers to reading books and articles on the subject and even hiding inside the back of a panel truck that was parked on gang turf to "observe them without being observed." Before writing the chapter in which his protagonist, Hinton, walks through the subway tunnel between the 96th and 110th Street stations, Yurick reportedly made the 14-block trip himself through near-total darkness. Having been raised in an immigrant household during the Great Depression by parents who were communists and trade-union activists, he seized on the idea of mixing Marxism with neo-Darwinism for the story's political subtext. Once all the prep work was done and the story outlined, it took him three weeks to write the entire novel.

The Warriors takes place over the course of 15 hours, beginning on the 4th of July. Instead of a name or number, Yurick starts each chapter with a time frame. An editor at Holt, Rinehart & Winston chose the opening quotes from Xenephon.

"Soldiers, you must not be downhearted because of recent events. I can assure you that there are as many advantages as disadvantages in what has happened."

"My friends, these people whom you see are the last obstacle which stops us from being where we have so long struggled to be. We ought, if we could, to eat them up alive."

—from *Anabasis* by Xenophon

July 4th, 11:10 P.M.

Six members of the Coney Island Dominators—Hector, Hinton, Lunkface, Bimbo, The Junior, and Dewey—are hiding out in a cemetery and wondering what has happened to their leader, Papa Arnold. They all wear hats except Lunkface, who has just lost his in an altercation. Bimbo is the bearer, armorer and treasurer of the gang. Hinton is the spray-paint artist. Dewey and the Junior are soldiers. Lunkface provides muscle.

The Dominators considers themselves a Family. Papa Arnold is Father and his woman is Mother. Hector, the second in command, is Uncle. The other gang members are Brothers and their girlfriends are Daughters and Sisters. Friends in the outer circle are Cousins, Nieces, and Nephews.

Hinton is curled up in the shadowed doorway of a tomb, fighting off sleep. The Junior wants to leave the cemetery because he thinks the dead rise from their graves at midnight, but Hector says they should stay in case Papa Arnold shows up. The Junior disagrees: "No one elected you father." Hector responds, "You want to tangle about it? Someone has got to be the father till we get back home."

July 4th, 3:00-4:30 P.M.

Members of the Delancey Thrones, including War-Counselor and Secretary, are hanging out in their clubhouse waiting for something big to begin. Their leader, Ismael Rivera, usually forbids them to have sex for a week before a rumble so they will be mean, but they seem prepared for something else today. Mannie Bernstein, the youth board worker assigned to the gang, meekly enters the clubhouse and tries to find out what they're up to, but this tight-lipped bunch offers him nothing but contempt. On the radio they hear "for all the boys and girls of the Paradise Social and Athletic Club, these grooves...it's *los Beatles*, boys and girls, banging out..." The Beatles song is a signal for the gangs to hit the streets.

July 4th, 7:00-10:30 P.M.

The Dominators march through the turf of the Colonial Lords. Papa Arnold shows the leader of the Lords an invitation from Ismael as a through-pass. One of the Lords, Willie, is obnoxious and almost starts a fight with Lunkface, but the pass is honored and the Dominators are allowed to march through. At the subway station, Bimbo buys 14 tokens, seven to get them to the Bronx and seven for the return trip. He also gives the others $7 each as "bread crumbs" to help them find their way back in case they get separated.

Their destination: Van Cortlandt Park in the Bronx, where Ismael has summoned "a thousand strong" from "almost every major fighting gang in the city." At the meeting place, a member of the Delancey Thrones, Benny, is leading the various gangs across the road that cuts through the park. He once lived on Dominators turf and had a run-in with Hector, which Lunkface tries to reignite but Papa Arnold quickly quells.

July 4th, 10:30-10:50 P.M.

Ismael begins talking softly and his words are passed among the "warriors" in the crowd via three signal men who relay what he's saying conversationally to those around them. The point of his meeting: There are 20,000 hardcore gang members in New York City—40,000 counting regular affiliates and 60,000 "unorganized but ready-to-fight"—which is about four army divisions, and if women are counted, then the number is up around 100,000. Since there are only 20,000 cops, "One gang could rule the city."

Somewhere in the crowd, a fight breaks out and guns are drawn. When the police arrive, many gang members suspect Ismael of setting them up and they shoot him. A riot ensues.

July 4th, 10:45-11:10 P.M.

Hector leads the Dominators out of the chaos. Along the way, Papa Arnold stops to look at Ismael's corpse and is jumped by several of the Delancey Thrones. The other Dominators unknowingly leave him behind to be beaten up.

July 4th, 11:10-11:45 P.M.

"Coney Island is 15 miles away; it might as well be fifteen hundred, because everyone between here and home is ready to come down on you."

Back in the cemetery where the novel begins, Hector is elected temporary Father in Papa Arnold's absence. He tells everyone to take out their membership pins so he can affix them to their hats to identify themselves as Coney Island Dominators. Several of the members complain that they will look too much like a gang with the pins on, but Hector insists. Their goal is to either get to a subway station and catch the train home or find a pay phone and call Wallie, their youth board worker, to come get them. As they leave, Hinton sprays their gang mark on a tombstone: "Dominators, LAMF, DTK." (Back then, a gang's name and the acronym for "Like a Mother Fucker, Down to Kill" was a common graffiti tag to tauntingly leave on a rival gang's turf.)

July 4th-July 5th, 11:40 P.M.-12:45 A.M.

The Dominators climb down the cemetery wall to the street below and Hector calls Wallie, who already knows about the rumble in the Bronx. He agrees to come get them. Hector is paranoid and thinks the cops are closing in. Lunkface teases two young couples passing by and suggests the gang steal the girls and rape them. Hector tells him to masturbate instead, and Lunkface does just that. A train arrives, and they jump the turnstiles to catch it.

July 5th, 12:45-1:30 A.M.

The other riders on the subway are almost zombie-like, and the Dominators can't figure out what is wrong with them until Hinton realizes they are gambling addicts on the way home from Yonkers Raceway. (They remind him of his mother's boyfriend, who is a bad gambler, as well as his half-brother Alonso, a junkie.) When they reach 225th Street, Hector tells the Junior to look at the subway map to ascertain their whereabouts.

Their train stops because of track repairs and the six Dominators get caught in a rush to the ticket booth for bus transfers. They miss the bus and are spotted by three warriors, one of whom leaves to find reinforcements. Hector is angry at the Junior for not knowing where they are, and decides to parley with the Bronx gang for safe passage.

July 5th, 1:30-2:30 A.M.

Hector meets with a member of the Borinquen Blazers, a Puerto Rican gang, while a young prostitute watches the proceedings and sizes up the

Dominators. The two warriors compare newspaper clippings—the Dominators have been written up in the *Daily News*, the Blazers in *La Prensa*. Hector mentions their youth board worker, and the Blazer admits they don't have one...yet. He agrees to let the Dominators through, and even tells them to avoid the Castro Stompers and the Jackson Street Masai on the way to the subway station. The negotiations unravel, however, when the prostitute demands the gang pin on Hector's hat as a gift and he refuses to give it to her.

The Dominators take off, followed by the Blazer and the prostitute, and pause a few blocks away to smoke, finish their booze and get pumped up and angry for the inevitable fight. Hinton brings up the rear while the Junior goes one block ahead to scout. The other Dominators push on, keeping an eye out for possible weapons and staying clear of the side streets so they don't get ambushed or attacked from above. They reach the Freeman Street station, but it's closed. Hector decides they better take care of the Blazers, which they do quickly and easily. The prostitute sticks with them, and on the way to the next subway station they see graffiti for the Castro Stompers and another gang called the Intervale Avenue Lesbos. Lunkface picks a fight with a passerby, and all six Dominators take turns stabbing the man while the prostitute screams that she wants a turn, too. Instead of giving her the knife, they gang-rape her on top of the fresh corpse and then leave her.

July 5th, 2:30-3:00 A.M.

While waiting for a train, Lunkface and Dewey get into an argument over who made the prostitute scream more during her sexual assault, which they settle with a literal pissing match (Hinton wins by pissing the farthest). They board the next train that arrives. The Junior reads a comic book that is about "ancient soldiers, Greeks, heroes who had to fight their way home through many obstacles, but in the end they made it." Hector, Dewey and Lunkface play a game involving a candy bar that has fallen on the floor. Following Hector's instructions, Lunkface punishes Hinton for a minor infraction by smoking his war cigarette and purposely getting ash on his hat. The six play chicken by hanging their heads out of the window, to see who is the manliest of the group. The one who comes closest to bashing their head against the tunnel wall is the winner and referred to as the Man with the Most Heart (Hinton wins this contest also). The Junior reaches the part in his comic book where the Greek soldiers see the sea. "The heroes were, the Junior could see, the hardest men in a hard world, admirable but, he thought, he wouldn't like to be in their place, even though he envied their adventures."

July 5th, 3:00-3:10 A.M.

The express train pulls into the 96th Street station, and the Dominators wait for the local. A transit cop spots them and lingers, keeping his eyes on them. He gets on the train, the six Dominators slip out as the doors slam shut, and the cop gets stuck on the train as it leaves, but another cop appears and gives chase. Hinton jumps off the platform and runs into the subway tunnel on the downtown line. Dewey and the Junior flee to another part of the station. Hector, Lunkface, and Bimbo jump onto the tracks, cross over to the uptown platform, run to the other end of it and go upstairs to the street.

July 5th, 3:10-3:35 A.M.

Hinton has a panic attack while wandering through the pitch darkness of the subway tunnel but eventually sees light coming from the next station, 110th Street. He makes it there and catches a downtown train.

July 5th, 3:10-3:35 A.M.

Dewey and the Junior escape the wheezing transit cop and hide on an uptown train. They pass the 100th, 116th, 125th, and 137th Street stations. The Junior reads his comic book and Dewey tries to figure out a plan to get back to Times Square to get the BMT to Coney Island. They both read the comic and talk about the Greek haircrest helmets and how they are similar to the gang pins and hats worn by the Dominators.

Although the Classics Illustrated comic books were popular in the States, their Xenophon adaptation (which the Junior reads in *The Warriors*) was only published in the U.K.

July 5th, 3:10-3:35 A.M.

Hector, Lunkface, and Bimbo run upstairs to 93rd Street and Broadway and flee toward the Hudson River. Lunkface removes his three-point Mercedes Benz pin, the mark of the Family, because he feels it is attracting too much attention from the police. Hector balks at this and the two nearly trade blows, but Hector finds a way to agree without losing face. They remove their pins and proceed as three similarly dressed young men—"squares"—having lost the identity of oneness. Lunkface is immediately regretful.

Walking through Riverside Park, the three encounter a drunk nurse on a park bench. Lunkface wants to rape her, but she finds Hector attractive and goes with him into the bushes to have sex. When Bimbo attempts to steal money from her purse, she begins screaming "Rape!" The police arrive and arrest all three gang members. Hector tries to explain that the nurse gave them the come-on, but the cops beat him up and break his nose.

July 5th, 3:45-4:30 A.M.

Hinton gets off at the Times Square station and doesn't see any of the other Dominators. He eats a lot of junk food, walks around 42nd Street, has sex with a $3 prostitute in the subway women's room, and goes three rounds against a Mr. Top Gun mechanical quick-draw shooting game in the Times Square arcade. Homosexuals hit on him. A seven-year-old boy tries to get money from him for dope. Eventually he reunites with the Junior and Dewey on the subway platform, and they board a train for home.

July 5th, 4:30-5:20 A.M.

On the subway, two high school couples in fancy evening clothes get on and sit across from them. The young men are muscular jocks who look at Hinton and the others with derision. Hinton imagines marrying a young woman like the ones across from him, settling down, owning a house, raising children and holding down an executive-position job that would require him to boss people around. When the two couples get off at Avenue J, the jocks give the three Dominators a last put-down look. Hinton, Dewey, and the Junior finally arrive at Coney Island, but they still have to cross through Colonial Lords turf to get home. Hinton wants to make it a raid. The other two are tired, but reluctantly go with him. They shout for the Lords to come outside and fight, and when none of them do, the three Dominators spray-paint obscene graffiti all over the Lords' turf.

July 5th, 5:20-6:00 A.M.

Hinton leads Dewey and the Junior to the beach, where they frolic in the water before heading to a candy store where the girlfriends of Hector, Bimbo, Dewey, and the Junior are still hanging out. The three learn that Papa Arnold returned hours ago. Hector's and Bimbo's girlfriends comfort each other after hearing that their men are missing. Dewey and the Junior go off with their girlfriends. Hinton wishes he had a girlfriend to be with right now. When he gets home, which he calls The Prison, his junkie brother Alonso is awake and listening to their mother and her boyfriend having sex in the stiflingly hot apartment. A baby is crying. Hinton crawls out onto the fire escape, curls into a ball with a thumb in his mouth, and goes to sleep.

After numerous arguments between Yurick and his editor over the language, violence and sexual content in the novel—the majority of which were won by Yurick—*The Warriors* was published by Holt, Rinehart & Winston in late summer 1965 and received favorable reviews overall. "Could it be that Sol Yurick whose first novel is so graphic and poignant, so hideous and hopeless, could have achieved the miracle of boot-strap elevation from the worst possible oral and physical environment to become a welfare worker?" asked Laura Scott Meyers in the *El Paso Herald-Post*. "The speculation is not idle, because if this were true, it would lend great weight to the most incredible account we have ever read of human degradation."

"This novel is in the same genre as the social protest fiction of the thirties," commented Mary Ann Riley in the *Carroll* (Iowa) *Daily Times Herald*. "But where is the writer of vision who will offer us answers to the problems posted by the denizens of the 'asphalt jungles'?" Bob Sorensen of the *Minneapolis Tribune* called the novel "remarkably effective" and stated that it "does what a newsreel can do so well—take a hurried, staccato look at a social blot, in this case the teen-age gangs that prowl New York." Frank Farrara of the San Rafael, CA *Daily Independent Journal* proclaimed it "a brutally realistic account" by an author who "chills the uninitiated with a cold, hard look at violence."

"The word 'family' usually brings to mind a wholesome picture of a happy unit of people bonded by love and companionship," wrote Bob Dale in the San Antonio, TX *Express and News*. "In *The Warriors*, author Sol Yurick depicts a Coney Island gang of juveniles calling themselves the 'Family,' and the picture presented is far from wholesome and completely devoid of love in the normal family sense." In his Louisville, KY *Courier-Journal* review, Charles Alva Hoyt, a member of the English faculty at Bennett College in Millbrook, New York, referred to the novel as "clean, hard and sound, with no phony sentiment pro or con—a simple, cool, unimpassioned narrative which lightly refers to its model on occasion."

Carol Seidenberg in the White Plains, NY *Journal News* found parallels to Homer's *The Odyssey*, with the six members of the Coney Island Dominators trying "like Odysseus to get back to the sea, their turf." She even compared the subway riders returning from Yonkers Raceway at 1:30 a.m. to the land of the lotus-eaters, as "Yurick's 'Warriors' travel through treacherous lands fraught with similar pitfalls found in *The Odyssey*." Alan Pryce-Jones in the *Philadelphia Inquirer* proclaimed it "a masterly first novel...a tale as chilling as, and much closer to home than, *Lord of the Flies*."

"The path down which Mr. Yurick runs his narrative is Xenophon's *Anabasis*—the road back to Greece," Robert Hatch wrote in *The Nation*. "He dwells perhaps too insistently on this model—these Negro boys are not the illustrious remnants of a professional army; they are a tribal party, bound together by magic rites, disciplined by paternal authority." ("He was a bit unhappy with the notion of making a connection between 10,000 mercenaries and street gangs," Yurick said of Hatch in an interview with *Cineaste* editors Al Auster and Dan Georgakas 14 years later. "But that's how Athens solved its juvenile delinquency problem. It hired them out as mercenaries—those were 14 and 15 year-old kids wandering around Asia being led by their various generals.")

A Brutal, Unvarnished Look at Gang Warfare

Retreat to Brooklyn
Vivid Odyssey of Juveniles on the Run

A night to dismember

Teen-Age Gang Rule In New York? Why Not?

Meanwhile, Hatch's assertion that the Dominators are "Negro boys" is debatable. Yurick seems to purposely avoid the physical details of his characters until the sequence in Riverside Park, where the nurse's point of view tells us that Hector has "a beautiful face and blond, wavy hair curling down from his set-back hat." Bimbo and Lunkface are described as darker-skinned: "The short, squat one was a muddy light brown and had a little fuzzy moustache and looked Indian-faced. The other one was bulky-big, ugly, Negro-faced." When Lunkface slips his arm around the nurse and tries to squeeze her breast, she tells him "Get away, Nigger." He is stunned for a moment, and thinks to himself he is American, "a Puerto Rican of Spanish descent." Going by that passage, it certainly sounds like the Dominators are a mixed gang, but in his introduction to the 2003 edition Yurick claims otherwise: "In the movie the Warriors were racially mixed; almost an impossibility. My warriors had all been black."

In the novel, the only explicitly "all black" gang is the one described from the point of view of a nervous, bigoted cop who encounters them as they walk to the subway, on their way to the meeting in the Bronx. "What were Negroes doing in this neighborhood? They all wore many little brass buckles on their raincoats and point-up shoes. Their hair was straightened, pompadoured high, held in place by wide, shiny black headbands." There's no confusing this gang for the Coney Island Dominators, who are described 10 pages earlier: "The men wore blue, paisley-print, button-down-collar shirts and too-tight black chino pants, high-crowned narrow-brimmed straw hats with their signs: cracked-off Mercedes-Benz hubcab ornaments—hard to come by—with safety pins soldered in the school shop to the three-ray halo stars."

'Warriors' on Film

American International has concluded co-production arrangements with Dennis Sanders and Robert Fresco for filming of the Sol Yurick novel, "The Warriors."

Sanders, Fresco To Try 'Warriors'

HOLLYWOOD — American International has concluded co-production arrangements with Dennis Sanders and Robert Fresco for filming of the Sol Yurick novel, "The Warriors."

AIP Buys Movie, Book Rights For 1970 Movie Schedule

In the decade and a half between the publication of *The Warriors* and the release of Walter Hill's movie, rumors circulated that several filmmakers (including Otto Preminger) were interested in bringing Yurick's novel to the big screen. The only deal that was widely reported in the trades came in November 1968, when American International Pictures concluded co-production arrangements with Denis Sanders and Robert M. Fresco for a film adaptation of the novel. It was one of several literary acquisitions AIP made following the arrival of Lawrence Gordon as their new vice president of production development.

Prior to the late '60s, AIP had relied on authors of classic literature—Edgar Allan Poe, Jules Verne, Nathaniel Hawthorne—for their occasional stabs at respectability, with a few exceptions (such as Richard Matheson, who they employed as a screenwriter). An attempt to produce a film from Philip Roth's novel *Letting Go*, touted as a collaboration of actor Peter Mark Richman and director Harvey Hart, ended in a lawsuit. However, *Paxton Quigley's Had the Course* by Stephen H. Yafa was produced as Richard Wilson's *Three in the Attic* (1968) and was a hit for AIP.

Perhaps this success was what led the studio to move on *The Warriors* and several other books, including *Public Parts and Private Places* by Robin Cook, *Venus Examined* by Robert Kyle, *The Adulteress* by William Maidment, and *Implosion* by D.F. Jones. Two more that were acquired during this time—Peter Saxon's *The Disorientated Man* and Angus Hall's *The Late Boy Wonder*—became Gordon Hessler's *Scream and Scream Again* (1970) and Theodore J. Flicker's *Up in the Cellar* a.k.a. *Three in the Cellar* (1970), respectively. The rest were never produced, though screenplays were commissioned for all of them (Matheson wrote the adaptation of *Implosion*).

Described as "a topical drama of today's social mores and trends in the nation's large cities," *The Warriors* was to be directed by Sanders and produced by Fresco, "with extensive if not exclusive locations in New York City," according to an article in the *Reno Evening Gazette and Nevada State Journal*. An acclaimed documentary filmmaker, Sanders and his brother Terry had won an Academy Award (Best Short Subject, Two-reel) in 1955 for *A Time Out of War*, which led to the siblings co-writing the screenplay adaptation for Raoul Walsh's *The Naked and the Dead* (1958), based on Norman Mailer's novel. Denis went on to direct *Crime and Punishment U.S.A.* (1959), *War Hunt* (1962)—the debut of Sydney Pollack and Tom Skerritt and first credited film role of Robert Redford—*One Man's Way* (1964), *Shock Treatment* (1964), and episodes of *Naked City*, *The Defenders*, *Route 66*, and *Mannix*. Fresco had entered the film business in the '50s as a writer for television and Universal creature features like Jack Arnold's *Tarantula* (1955) and John Sherwood's *The Monolith Monsters* (1957) before hooking up with Sanders.

In April 1969, a news item announced that Shane Stevens had been tapped to write the *Warriors* screenplay, a smart decision on AIP's part since Stevens' first novel, *Go Down Dead*, was a contemporary gang tale set in Harlem that had garnered some praise and attention two years earlier. It tells the incredibly sordid story of 16-year-old African-American gang leader Adam Clayton Henry, "King" of the Playboys, who peddles dope, pimps out young girls and performs in a pornographic movie in order to raise the "bread" to arm his Playboys with enough dynamite to blast their Caucasian counterparts, the Tigers, into next week's garbage. *The New York Times*' James R. Frakes wrote that, compared to this book, "James Baldwin sounds like Edith Wharton, and even LeRoi Jones seems prissy."

No reasons were ever reported for the collapse of the AIP deal, but it might have been something as simple as artistic differences between exploitation-minded AIP heads Samuel Z. Arkoff and James H. Nicholson and purposeful documentarians Fresco and Sanders, whose *Czechoslovakia 1918-1968* (1969) earned the 1970 Academy Award for Best Documentary, Short Subject. Instead of doing *The Warriors*, the two collaborated again on *Trial: The City and County of Denver vs. Lauren R. Watson*, a four-part, six-hour documentary chronicling the criminal proceedings against Black Panther member Watson that was produced for National Educational Television (NET) in the fall of 1970. Sanders also made the music documentaries *Elvis: That's the Way It Is* (1970) and *Soul to Soul* (1971) and the low-budget horror feature *Invasion of the Bee Girls* (1973).

Stevens went on to write other high-profile novels, but never saw any of them achieve best-seller status or become motion pictures, though one

Yurick's novel, republished as movie tie-in editions in the U.S. and Italy.

came close and is now considered a classic of the thriller genre. *By Reason of Insanity*, about a serial killer who believes he is the offspring of real-life criminal Caryl Chessman and one of his rape victims, received a huge push from publisher Simon & Schuster in 1978 that resulted in Columbia Pictures purchasing the movie rights at auction for $500,000 and Dell grabbing the paperback rights for a high six-figure sum. Stephen King called it "One of the finest novels ever written about perfect evil" and later named Thad Beaumont's literary creation in *The Dark Half*, Alexis Machine, after a character in another Stevens crime novel, *Dead City*.

As for Yurick, it would be another nine years before the Marxist author would see his ideological work brought to the screen, albeit with the class politics and hostility largely absent and a cast of actors 10 to 15 years older than the characters in the novel. "The movie is an evisceration and distortion of the book," he complained to the editors of *Cineaste*, before admitting that the money he was paid for the movie rights was needed if he wanted to continue writing and living. Years later, he confessed to secretly hoping "the violence and controversy surrounding the movie would help sell the movie, thus generating demand for the reprinting of my book, which it did."

2 Shooting After Dark: Making *The Warriors*

Following its aborted adaptation by American International Pictures (see Chapter One), *The Warriors* found a new lease on screen life thanks to producer Lawrence Gordon's partnership with director Walter Hill. During his AIP days, Gordon had been impressed with Hill's screenplays and invited him to direct one for that company; when Gordon subsequently accepted a deal to make low-budget genre fare for Columbia Pictures, his first film for the studio was Hill's *Hard Times* (1975)—though that one was based on an original script by Bryan Gindoff and Bruce Henstell that Hill rewrote. The director and Gordon re-teamed on the Ryan O'Neal-starring neo-noir thriller *The Driver* (1978), and then began prepping a Western called *The Last Gun*, which Hill had written with Roger Spottiswoode (who would co-script the director's 1982 hit *48 HRS.*).

They were eight weeks away from shooting *The Last Gun* when Britain's EMI Films, which was backing the project, pulled the financing. Gordon had commissioned a *Warriors* screenplay by David Shaber, a Yale Drama School graduate and playwright with a few big- and small-screen credits to his name, and had sent that and Sol Yurick's novel to the director, who initially believed the project was "too extreme and too weird" for any studio to let them make it. When *The Last Gun* fell apart, Gordon took a shot at mounting *The Warriors*. "We were scrambling looking for a picture and Larry thought he might be able to get *The Warriors* on at Paramount because they were interested in youth movies," Hill recalled to TheFader.com's Eric Ducker.

Once Paramount agreed to produce *The Warriors*, Hill set about refining Shaber's script to suit his own tastes. "The screenplay was solid," the director said in Paramount's production notes, "but I began to get interested in other ideas in the story, particularly in its allegorical aspects. I eventually wound up rewriting a lot of it. The novel is a bit more realistic than the film in its portrait of the gang subculture. We essentially converted that realism and used the gang mainly as a convention to tell a different kind of story. You'll find that the film sets up and works within its own fantasy world."

The director initially wanted to populate that world solely with black and Hispanic actors, but Paramount nixed that idea, citing commercial concerns. Still, for authenticity's sake, *The Warriors* was cast entirely out of New York; actors considered for the movie who wound up not appearing in it included everyone from Robert De Niro to Tony Danza. At the time, Danza was a Golden Gloves boxer embarking on an acting career, and he invited Hill and his producers to one of his bouts—in which he KO'ed his opponent, Billy Perez. "I just kill this guy, knock him through the ring ropes into the first row," Danza told Deadline.com's Mike Fleming Jr. "I am king, just walking around like King Kong and my eyes meet Larry Gordon, who's standing on the floor in my corner and who says, that's the greatest audition I've ever seen." Danza was awarded the role of Cowboy in *The Warriors*, but at the same time, he got an audition with TV mogul James L. Brooks, and decided to drop out of the film in favor of what would be his star-making role in the sitcom *Taxi*.

Chosen for what was supposed to be the lead role of The Fox was Thomas G. Waites, who had recently shot his film debut as a prison-gang leader in *On the Yard* (1979)—and had been part of a real gang during his early years in Pennsylvania. "Where I grew up, it wasn't like it is today," Waites says. "There were no guns or anything like that. It was just sort of out of survival; people clustered in groups, and ours was called the Bristol Terrorist gang, because that was the neighborhood that we hung out in—a place called Bristol, PA, on the Delaware River. We did get into a few rumbles with other gangs, but it only lasted for me from when I was around 12 to 14, because I got hit by a car very seriously, and that took me out of the streets and the gang for good."

Tony Danza preferred to drive a *Taxi* over riding the subways with *The Warriors*.

A rising young star, he was courted for both *The Warriors* and Warner Bros.' similarly themed *The Wanderers* (1979)—Philip Kaufman's adaptation of Richard Price's novel—and chose the former. "Scott Rudin, who went on to be a producer, was at this time a casting director, and a very successful one," Waites says. "He took me out to dinner and said, 'You know, you're going to be offered these two movies tomorrow, so you better think about which one you want to do.' I said, 'Can we put them off?' and he said, 'No, they've got to know.' But I bought myself a few days and hung out with Walter, and he screened *Rebel Without a Cause* for me, and we agreed that the James Dean character was something that I was going to try to go for as Fox. So I turned down *The Wanderers* [for which he was offered Turkey, the part ultimately played by Alan Rosenberg] because I thought Walter had more of a vision. And it turns out he did."

Another of the film's stars was discovered when Hill, who was part of the producing team on *Alien* (1979), watched a shot-in-Israel thriller called *Madman* (1978) to check out Sigourney Weaver's performance. Mi chael Beck, who had also appeared in the hit TV miniseries *Holocaust* (1978), was *Madman*'s lead, and Hill was impressed enough to give him the part of Swan.

A few hours after he was cast in *The Warriors*, Beck separated his shoulder in a bicycle accident and was told by an orthopedist not to use

Thomas Waites as the ill-fated the Fox.

his left arm for at least a week. That was on a Friday afternoon, and the actor had a lunch meeting scheduled with Hill on the following Monday. To conceal his injury, Beck hooked his thumb in the pocket of his waistcoat vest and left it there for the entire meal. "The arm was not moving," Beck told *Shock Cinema* magazine's Paul Talbot, "and I wasn't about to tell [Hill] because for insurance reasons, or whatever, they may have booted me from the film."

James Remar, who had also debuted in *On the Yard*, put on a physical show for the *Warriors* team that helped land him the part of Ajax. Auditioning with the scene in which Ajax is handcuffed to a park bench by the undercover policewoman, and struggles to get free, "I grabbed ahold of a corner of this huge conference table, making like it was the bench," Remar describes on the *Warriors* Ultimate Director's Cut DVD. "I really just pulled against it and got enraged with this whole situation. And in the middle of the reading, I really pull on the thing and lifted the whole cor-

Michael Beck as Swan.

ner of this conference table up that weighed hundreds of pounds—I was quite strong at the time!" Hill later cast Remar in his Western *The Long Riders* (1980) and in perhaps his best-known role as psychopathic criminal Albert Ganz in *48 HRS.*, as well as *Wild Bill* (1995). Remar also initially played Corporal Dwayne Hicks in *Aliens* (1986), on which Hill was an executive producer, but was replaced early in the shoot with Michael Biehn.

"Walter has always trusted my choices as an actor," Remar told *Shock Cinema*'s Jeremiah Kipp. "Being with him feels like I'm with an old friend, and I understand what he's saying and what he wants from me. I think it's that I saw his writing and understood the force that he wanted it expressed with. When I stepped up and said some of those lines with a real 'fuck you' kind of force, like 'Go fuck yourself,' and really meant it, he liked that."

For the part of the police decoy in Riverside Park who busts Ajax, the producers chose Mercedes Ruehl, whose résumé listed a lot of regional

James Remar, sporting the most blood you'll see in *The Warriors*, as Ajax.

theater credits but no screen roles. Three months after *The Warriors* was released, her best friend and college roommate, journalist Madeleine Blais, detailed Ruehl's experience on the film in a *Washington Post* profile. "Mercedes said she had studied the script last summer when the filming took place and was somewhat appalled by the cheapness of the language, but against her better instincts (and probably in light of the $1,200 she would earn) decided to give it a try." In the same article, Ruehl herself summed up her motion picture debut as "a smart part with loathsome lines in a film whose overall integrity I doubt." After this questionable start, Ruehl ultimately achieved fame and acclaim for her performances on stage, film, and TV, including a Tony Award (*Lost in Yonkers*, 1991) and an Academy Award (*The Fisher King*, 1992), while Blais would go on to win the Pulitzer Prize for Feature Writing ("Zepp's Last Stand," *The Miami Herald*) less than a year later.

Nonetheless, the decoy role was a challenge for the first-time screen actress. "An old acting coach once advised her to give any scene the highest stakes possible," Blais wrote, "and her subtext for how to interpret the role of this decoy was that it is the girl's first time out as a decoy: 'I would make her a little awkward, a little funny, very relieved and proud when she finally catches this guy.' " Hill disagreed, advising her to play the part "cool as a prostitute." The outcome, Ruehl told Blais, was a lesson in compromise: "...if you want to do something one way and your director wants to do it another way, you have to come up with a third approach you can both live with."

The filmmakers had been seeking a Hispanic actress for Mercy, the Bronx girl who joins the Warriors on their trek, but Deborah Van Valkenburgh, who had appeared in the Broadway revival of *Hair*, won them over during the course of the audition process. "Her character has probably the greatest transition in attitude of anyone in the film," Hill says on the DVD, "and she pulled it off, I thought, with tremendous style." Although she wasn't required on set until nearly a month after shooting began, Van

Mercedes Ruehl as the undercover cop.

Valkenburgh spent a week beforehand hanging out with the cast and crew to get used to the nocturnal schedule. "There's a tribal feeling about this film, and I felt really close to all the guys," she says in the production notes. "Even if I wasn't needed, I wanted to be on the set because I belonged with my fellow actors." Van Valkenburgh wound up suffering a couple of injuries while filming *The Warriors*: First she fell down a flight of subway stairs and broke her wrist, which necessitated Mercy donning a jacket to cover the actress' cast midway through the film ("I stole it," she explains to Swan, and that's that) and later, Beck accidentally bopped her in the eye with a baseball bat.

Deborah Van Valkenburgh as Mercy with Michael Beck as Swan.

Off-Broadway actor Brian Tyler auditioned, did screen tests, and read numerous times to get the role of Snow, a character who didn't even speak until the final scene in the original screenplay. Dorsey Wright had just been interviewed in *The New York Times* about his role as Hud in Milos Forman's film of *Hair* (1979) when he was cast as Cleon, the leader of the Warriors and the first character seen in the movie. He's also the first Warrior to exit the movie, when he's elbowed into submission by the Gramercy Riffs at the 15-minute mark.

Tom McKitterick had appeared in an off-Broadway production of Eugene O'Neill's *The Great God Brown* and recently been cast in NBC's doomed daytime drama *For Richer, For Poorer* shortly before auditioning for *The Warriors*. He did one reading and was hired, but as he explained to Gareth Jones of The Warriors Movie Site, "Originally I was to play another role, with Tony Danza cast as Cowboy. He left to do another project and I was assigned to his role."

The casting process was not as easy for Terry Michos, who had been in a national touring company production of *Grease* for nine months playing one of the T-Birds (in a cast headed by Peter Gallagher as Danny and Gail Edwards as Sandy) when he auditioned for Hill and executive producer Frank Marshall. Much to his amazement, since he had no movie or television experience, Michos was called back for a second audition and found

Terry Michos as Vermin.

himself among the twelve finalists chosen to fill the roles of the nine Warriors. He remembers, "They brought us all up to the Gulf + Western Building" on Columbus Circle, where Paramount Pictures was headquartered. "They sized us up, put us next to each other—what they were doing was matching looks, but I didn't know that at the time. I was thinking, 'Wow, I'm in.' "

That feeling of accomplishment didn't last long, though. "A week later, my agent called and said, 'They don't want you for *The Warriors*. They're going in a different direction.' I was heartbroken. I went to dinner with my girlfriend and I just cried." Michos returned to the *Grease* roadshow for a few more performances, but was summoned back to New York by his agent with the promise of one more shot at nabbing a role in *The Warriors*. The reason for the callback? Danza's departure for *Taxi*, which necessitated the hiring of a new, certain 'type.' McKitterick, who had been cast as Vermin, moved into the Cowboy role vacated by Danza, but as Michos explains, "They weren't matching Tony Danza against Tom McKitterick. Tony Danza was the guy who bumped me out, so the matchup was Tony Danza left and I came back in, because all the guys that were interviewed when I was in that office were that type—y'know, 5-foot-10, 5-foot-11, muscular, Italian-looking, nice-looking... I'm not saying I'm nice-looking, I'm just trying to make a point—that they were looking for a Tony Danza type." And they evidently found him with Michos, since he was ultimately cast in the role of Vermin.

The showiest turn in *The Warriors* is that of David Patrick Kelly as Luther, the deranged leader of the Rogues who shoots Cyrus and pins the murder on our heroes. Discovered by Hill and Gordon in a play called *Working*, in which he portrayed a hippie with passive-aggressive tendencies, Kelly adopted a Method approach to Luther, never interacting with his co-stars playing the Warriors. He would also become a Hill regular, once again playing a creep named Luther in *48 HRS.* and appearing in *Last Man Standing* (1996); *Warriors* associate producer Joel Silver brought Kelly back when he produced *Commando* (1985)—in which Kelly receives

David Patrick Kelly as Luther.

Arnold Schwarzenegger's most memorable sign-off line ("Remember, Sully, when I promised to kill you last? I lied!")—and *The Adventures of Ford Fairlane* (1990).

"David is such an intense actor," says Joel Weiss, who plays the driver of the Rogues' hearse (initially named Butcher Boy before being rechristened as Cropsey). "He's a mime, he plays drums, and in the morning he would do tai chi, and everybody would be looking at him strange. He kept away from people, because that's how Luther is; he didn't talk to any of the Rogues, only in character, so when we shot, that was the real deal. But I got along with him great, because we were in tune. We didn't have to rehearse. You know the scene at the gas station? One take. You know why? All that stuff between David and I wasn't in the script. He would do stuff, and I just went with it."

Kelly brought his friend and sometime co-star Lynne Thigpen onto the film to play the DJ who keeps the other gangs apprised of the Warriors' movements—and he reported that Thigpen was startled when she saw that only close-ups of her mouth are used in the final film, to emphasize her "evocative" voice. Thigpen got to show her face in Hill's subsequent *Streets of Fire* (1984), in which Van Valkenburgh also appears.

Like Waites, Weiss had a choice to make between *The Warriors* and *The Wanderers*. "I'd been hearing about *The Warriors* for a long time from different actors, and they were all telling me, 'You're perfect for it,'" he remembers. "But my mind was on *The Wanderers*. I read the book 22 times, and I wanted to be in that movie.

"So finally, I went for [a *Warriors*] audition. I went to the Gulf + Western building, dropped two names, got to the 24th floor, and went to the secretary and said, 'I'm Joel Weiss, I'm here to see Walter Hill.' Now, I saw *Hard Times* when I was in college, and I said, 'He's gonna be the first director who ever directs me in a motion picture.' I saw everything he did. The secretary said, 'If you're looking to read the script, it's upstairs,' and

Lynne Thigpen—all you see of her—as the DJ.

I said, 'No, I have an appointment with Walter Hill.' 'Uh, I don't see your name on here.'

"Today, you'd get handcuffed, you'd be arrested," Weiss laughs. "But she called up the casting director, and he got on the phone and said, 'Joel Weiss, what are you doing up there?' I said, 'You only go around once in life, and you got to grab for all the gusto.' There was this pause, and he said, 'Good luck.' So she said to me, 'You're gonna have to leave,' but she was nice about it. Then all of a sudden I heard a voice: 'Martha, come in here.' And she did, and came out with papers. She walked by me, made a little motion, and I stood right up and walked into Walter Hill's office. I said, 'Walter, I'm Joel Weiss, and I should be in your movie.' He wound up bringing me in to read, and I got the part! And Martha was Martha Schumacher, who became Martha De Laurentiis."

For Cyrus, the charismatic leader of the Gramercy Riffs who aspires to unite New York City's street tribes, the filmmakers originally pressed an actual gang leader into service. When he went missing without explanation shortly before filmmaking commenced, he was replaced with theater actor Roger Hill. He makes a commanding impression in his limited screen time—his exhortation "Can you dig it?!" is perhaps the movie's second most-quoted bit of dialogue—but sadly, he never landed another significant film assignment.

Another oft-quoted line—"We're gonna rain on you, Warriors!"—is heard during our heroes' fiery confrontation with the "real low class" Bronx gang, The Orphans. Decades later, Apache Ramos is still recognized as the Orphan who shouts this empty threat, and nowadays he writes it alongside his signature at fan conventions and other public appearances. "I had a wonderful girlfriend at the time [whose] brother was a known actor on Broadway, Treat Williams," Ramos says. "His girlfriend at the time, Janie Sell, was a Broadway actress, and they were so good to me. I was wearing one of Treat's shirts when I got my first 8x10 [headshot]."

Sell introduced Ramos to an agent who started sending him out on auditions, but without much success. "I was working at Bloomingdales when I got the call for *The Warriors*. So I went, reluctantly. I had on a black T-shirt with silver letters that said 'Bronx.' It was summertime, I was in shorts. I had my 8x10 and a little bottle of rum." He laughs and adds, "I don't recommend it to anybody." When he got to the Gulf + Western Building, he found a "a fucking million guys there, or it seemed that way. It just seemed like a whole bunch of dudes were there, and I couldn't care less."

Ramos found a spot in line and sat down. "I was sipping my rum and this white guy sat next to me and was talking to me. I offered him a taste, he said no, we talked, blah blah blah, and then he disappeared." When

Roger Hill as Cyrus.

Apache Ramos (at right) with his fellow Orphans.

Ramos' name was finally called to go in for the casting session, there was a surprise waiting for him. "That white guy who had been sitting next to me briefly? That was Walter Hill," he laughs. "He hired me immediately, on the spot. He just liked my vibe. He said, 'I wish I had met you sooner, but I do have a small part. Would you take it?' I said, 'Sure I'll take it!' And that's how I became Orphan #2."

Michael Garfield Levine, who won the part of one of the Rogues backing up Kelly's Luther and is credited as Michael Garfield, similarly remembers the cattle-call atmosphere. "There were a ton of people there because they were casting for several gangs, and it was sort of like showing up for Little League at the beginning of the season. You could see that they were rather quickly assigning various people to various gangs."

Puerto Rican-born Marcelino Sanchez had studied painting at the High School of Art and Design before Gordon spotted him during a casting session for *The Warriors* and offered him the role of Rembrandt. The day the movie opened in New York, Sanchez was one of the many local cast members who joined Gordon and Hill for a press conference in which the participants broke off into groups of three or four to answer questions. When *Boxoffice*'s John Cocchi asked him about the studio's decision to make so many of the film's young stars available at the same time for an "instant interview," Sanchez replied, "They got us all together because we're unknowns. But that won't be true in a few years."

Unfortunately, Sanchez never did land another role as substantial as Rembrandt, though he was seen regularly on *The Bloodhound Gang*, a serialized mystery segment of the PBS children's science show *3-2-1 Contact* (which also featured Ginny Ortiz, *The Warriors*' candy counter girl), and made guest appearances on *Hill Street Blues* and *CHiPs*. In 1982, Hill gave him a small role as the parking lot attendant in *48 HRS.*, in which he was reunited with Kelly and billed in the closing credits as James Marcelino. Tragically, Sanchez succumbed to AIDS-related cancer in November 1986. He was 28.

Marcelino Sanchez as Rembrandt.

"God rest his soul," Waites says of Sanchez. "So young, such a beautiful, promising talent and a lovely person. You know, these were really tough conditions; I mean, not Ukraine tough, but tough for a bunch of actors, and Marcelino never had a bad word to say about anything or anyone ever. He was just always keeping everyone's spirits up. He was a great kid."

The last of the nine Warriors to be cast was Cochise, which proved to be a tough role to fill. David Harris had just returned from Minneapolis, where he'd been appearing in a production of David Rabe's *Streamers*, when his agent in New York called him about a role in *The Warriors* that the producers were having a problem casting. "Walter Hill saw like, I don't know, three or four hundred actors...but he couldn't find Cochise," Harris told the hosts of The Five Count radio show on Mankato, MN's KMSU. A graduate of the High School of Performing Arts, Harris already had a leading role in the Emmy-nominated TV movie *Judge Horton and the Scottsboro Boys* (1976) on his list of credits, followed by two Broadway productions, *Secret Service* (with Meryl Streep and John Lithgow) and *Boy Meets Girl* (directed by Lithgow), and an appearance on the TV cop show *Kojak*. Still, he wasn't prepared for what happened during his meeting with Hill. "I walked into the room with Walter—I had two scenes to read for him, but he took one look at me and said, 'Go down to wardrobe.' "

Creating that wardrobe—clothing the laundry list of fictional gangs invented by Hill and Shaber—was a monumental task that fell to costume designer Bobbie Mannix, who had done two previous, much less sartorially varied features and has since been very busy in the commercials and music-video worlds. With no prior knowledge of the subject, she used her deep imagination to come up with distinctive outfits and looks (drawing inspiration from the rock band Kiss for the Baseball Furies' face paint), satisfying Hill's directive to make them look "strange."

"I read the script and thought it was great," Mannix says. "I didn't know about Sol Yurick or anything about gangs in New York at the time, but I quickly learned. I was given a list of 120 names of gangs that were in the preproduction notes, and it was my job to differentiate every one of them.

Well, at the time, everybody was done up in denim and black leather, and I said, 'That ain't gonna happen, because I have 120 gangs, 10 members deep, in the conclave.' So I had to separate them all, and I did it by color. I took the name of each gang, picked different colors for each one, and that's how it all started.

"I designed all the costumes and logos for all the gangs, as well as the makeup for the Baseball Furies," she reveals. "In those days, there wasn't such

From the Warriors' getup to the iconic visages of the Baseball Furies, Bonnie Mannix helped define the look of *The Warriors*.

a thing as makeup design and hair design. It was costume design, and since I was on before everybody else, I did the sketches for everything. I had all the patches made in California; even though I was sent to New York to work, I had those done in LA, and in those days, it was all done by hand."

Her outfits for the Lizzies, she remembers, were initially a little too revealing. "I had put makeup on the nipples and given them fishnet-type shirts that were all colored. And I think it became a little too risqué for a lot of them, so they wore jackets on top of their fishnet shirts."

Mannix's sometimes outlandish getups further establish Hill's New York as a fantasy world, disconnected from the real world of street toughs. "This movie was unique; it was crazy," she notes. "Real gangs don't dress like that; I made it all up. I mean, what gangs do you know that dress like mimes? What gangs do you know that dress like dancers?"

The Lizzies, in their less revealing outfits.

The actors playing the Warriors all wound up bonding during a production that encompassed 60 straight days of night shoots. Filming commenced on June 26, 1978, and the season put the filmmakers at a disadvantage, as they had to deal with the short summertime nights. (The cast were picked up in the evening and dropped off the following morning at the Gulf + Western Building.) In addition, there were several other pictures shooting in New York City at the same time, which made crewing up another difficulty. The original first assistant director wound up being fired early on, and David Sosna was brought in from Los Angeles to replace him.

"They had done a week of *The Warriors* and the New York first assistant director had made a mess of things," Sosna relates. "The neighborhood people were stealing from the trucks, they were dropping stuff from the rooftops to screw up the [filming]... He'd lost control of the neighborhood, largely because he'd been making inappropriate comments in response to the bad behavior. So I got a phone call from Joel Silver asking if I could go there, how quickly I could get there, so on and so forth. I showed up a couple of days later."

Not only was the Hollywood-based Sosna immediately faced with the new challenges of AD'ing a Manhattan shoot, he had to overcome the notion that LA ADs were too soft to handle the rigors of New York location filming. "There's a lot of hostility in the New York crews for California people," he admits. "In fact, Frank Marshall, who was the line producer, told me after I got there and after I'd done my first half day, 'When you have lunch, don't sit with us, sit with the New York crew. Otherwise, they'll peg you for a California guy.' " Sosna proved himself on *The Warriors*, and he too became part of Hill's team for *48 HRS.* and *Streets of Fire*.

Paramount, aware of numerous other similarly themed movies in the works, was in a race to get *The Warriors* out first. For Hill, a sense of urgency arose for another reason: *The Driver* opened on July 28 that summer to negative reviews and poor box-office returns. "I had the feeling that I wasn't going to last long as a director," Hill recalled to *The Village Voice*'s Jackson Connor, "so I wanted to get my licks in."

As the filmmaker has pointed out, *The Warriors* is unusual in the action genre in that it opens with by far its biggest setpiece: the nighttime rally in which Cyrus lays out his plan for the assembled gangs to join forces to take over the city. Roger Hill's magnetic delivery immediately grabs the audience's attention, and after he is shot, the cops arrive, and the scene devolves into chaos, the story is literally off and running.

"There actually was an event where every gang gathered in the Bronx, in I think 1972," Waites claims. "There's this grainy footage of it out there somewhere. This one dude called all the gangs together and said, 'There ain't but 3,700 cops, and there's 7,000 of us.' And they were like, '*Yeahhhh!*' And then the cops pulled in and broke it up. They were considering anarchy, I think, at that juncture."

Although set in Van Cortlandt Park in the Bronx, this setpiece was shot over several nights in Riverside Park on the Upper West Side of Manhattan. "I found that location," says Rob Ryder, who handled several jobs on *The Warriors*, including location scout, though he only received credit for playing a Baseball Fury. "That was a huge find for me because they were going crazy trying to figure out where they were going to shoot that [conclave scene]." Ryder had moved to New York after college, landed a contract to play professional basketball in Europe, and was training every day in various courts around the Big Apple when he met a wealthy financier who had put money into a low-budget crime film that was shooting in New Jersey. Through this investor, Ryder got a production assistant job on the film, which turned out to be *The Death Collector* (1976), remembered today for containing the big-screen debuts of Joe Pesci and Frank Vincent, and as the audition reel that got them higher-profile roles in *Raging Bull* (1980).

Ryder liked the experience so much that he called his sports agent and told him he was going to stay in New York and work on films instead of going to Europe to play basketball. John Stark, the production manager on *The Death Collector*, found work for Ryder on other movies and then hired him as a PA on *The Warriors*. "Within a couple of days, they bumped me up to location scout," he explains. "I spent the first few weeks running all over the city. That's when I found the conclave. I remembered Riverside Park from playing ball there. I took a whole bunch of Polaroids and ran them over to Walter and said, 'Check this out.' "

Once Ryder switched positions and stepped in front of the camera, his membership in the Screen Actors Guild became a point of contention. "I tried to hold onto my production job for a few days," he says, in a tone that acknowledges the big union no-no he was committing. "Everyone was looking at me sideways, like 'Dude, what are you trying to do? You're working all night, taking off the makeup and coming into the office to go scout locations?!' " The double-dipping only lasted a few days before a SAG representative caught on and complained to Sosna, who told Ryder to choose, right then and there, which side of the camera he was going to work on. Considering the money he was making and the fun he was having, the decision was a no-brainer. "I left the production job and finished up as a Fury, and then Walter asked me to be a Punk in the bathroom fight scene and I said, 'Sure!' That was fun, too."

Another stuntman who donned the Furies pinstripes was Steve James, several years before he rebranded himself as an '80s action star in Cannon productions like *The Delta Force* and the *American Ninja* movies. "I did a lot of stuntwork in New York," he explained to *M.A.M.A.: Martial Arts Movie Associates* writer Bill Connolly. "I was a member of a group called Stunt Specialists. My first professional job was *The Warriors*. I was a Baseball Fury."

"Steve James was a really cool guy, but he wasn't an active Fury," says Ryder. "He put on the makeup and uniform, but he wasn't in any of the Fury fights. I think he appeared in the conclave scene."

Even though he wasn't a participant, the fight scenes still made a big impression on James. "What I dug about *The Warriors* was the choreography of it," he told *M.A.M.A.* "Craig Baxley staged it just like it was a Shaw Brothers fight, with movement in the background and something going on in the foreground, so your eyes see a whole [panoramic] vision, and it's

Steve James in one of his best-known roles: Jackson in *American Ninja 2: The Confrontation.*

like movement, movement, movement, and it's quick cuts. It's one of the few times I've seen an American film with that kind of great choreography where your eyes are just moving all over the place."

Real gang members were cast as part of the crowd assembling for Cyrus' messianic speech, with off-duty police offers scattered among them to assure there wasn't any real-life trouble. According to comic book writer/artist Larry Hama (*G.I. Joe: A Real American Hero*, *Wolverine*), who briefly pursued a stage and screen acting career in the mid- to late 1970s, several members of the notorious Chinatown gang the Ghost Shadows were cast alongside him and other actors as the nine delegates of an all-Asian gang known as the Savage Huns. In between setups during the filming in Riverside Park, the production team would keep all of the gang members together in a holding area inside a playground. "They had about three hundred guys for this gang conference scene," Hama told interviewer Christopher Irving. "The Ghost Shadows decided, 'We're going to take this entire corner of the playground with swings and seesaws so we have somewhere to sit,' and forbade everybody else from going into that area. They stuck by it."

Can you spot the real gang members in this photo?

Getting real gang members together in one place and mingling them with actors, all of them wearing the outfits of fictional gangs created for the movie, was riskier than anyone wanted to admit. At the time, the Ghost Shadows were notorious for getting into often fatal shootouts with rival gangs, usually in and around the Pagoda Theater on East Broadway in Chinatown. One such altercation took place during the U.S. premiere of Bruce Lee's *Fist of Fury* on November 7, 1972, when three members of the Black Eagles stormed into the crowded lobby and opened fire, wounding the teenaged leader of the rival Ghost Shadows and killing one of his associates. The Ghost Shadows retaliated four months later by ambushing one of the Black Dragons outside the Pagoda, missing their target but striking a 71-year-old man twice in the back.

In 1976, two members of the Ghost Shadows were killed in another shootout inside the Pagoda, this time by the leader of the Flying Dragons. As a result, anyone in close proximity to real gang members while wearing the same "colors" during the conclave scene could've found themselves in harm's way. "What was worrisome was that the other gangs couldn't tell the difference between [the actors] and the Ghost Shadows," Hama said. "These guys came to the set with their .357 Magnums and nines tucked into their belts under the costumes."

"Most of the actors who were working on the film were scared ridiculous, because they were outnumbered," says David Copeland, an uncredited stunt player on the film. "I think for every 10 actors, they had 100 gang members. These were real gang members, guys from the street, and there were a lot of them. I think the guys who were playing the Warriors were afraid of getting challenged and things like that."

One of Sosna's responsibilities as the first AD was to actually gain control of this crowd and get them to follow direction. "I called out the biggest guy I could find and I called out a skinny guy in a wheelchair," he recalls. "They came up to me and I said to both guys, 'I'll give you a hundred bucks each in cash and you're done for the day if you just play along like I'm big and tough and you're afraid of me.' 'Oh yes, sir! A hundred dollars? Yes, sir!' I proceeded to chew them out loudly in front of the crowd about the terrible errors they had made, and how I would not tolerate deviations from my vision of what should happen, and I said, 'You're fired.' I pointed my finger very dramatically, and they went away. The crowd was suddenly afraid of me. Pretend fascism works for half an evening."

Garfield recalls a further problem that came up while shooting the conclave: "Because it was an outdoor location right on Riverside Drive—where, of course, everybody's building in the neighborhood faces the park—there were logistical concerns in terms of how many trucks were there, and how much noise we were making. Since it was so close to the residents, literally across the street, they got up in arms about the amount of noise. Like when Cyrus was on that tower, his voice carried throughout the neighborhood.

"People in the neighborhood finally got fed up with the amount of noise every night," he continues. "Shooting that went on for quite a few nights, and the neighborhood people put boomboxes in the windows of their apartment buildings and blasted them to disrupt the shoot, so the production would get the message that they were fed up with them. Walter Hill, if I'm not mistaken, got one of the producers to get a significant amount of cash and go and persuade these people, either by buying their boomboxes from them or by simply saying, 'We're sorry. Here's some money. Would you please not do that?' "

Another issue that arose was certain members of the crowd leaving the shoot while still wearing their costumes. "I remember seeing extras, at like 2 or 3 in the morning, walking home with our wardrobe on," Mannix says. "They wore crap clothes to the set, and then walked home with our clothes on. This was not good; they were stealing our costumes! They would come in with junk and instead of handing our outfits back to the wardrobe department, they'd walk off with them."

The solution, as cinematographer Andrew Laszlo recalled in his autobiography *Every Frame a Rembrandt*, was to issue raffle tickets to the extras as they put their outfits on, with the giveaway held after the night's filming was done and they returned the clothes. "This system worked well until the third or fourth morning, when the winner, happily carrying his new color TV set, was mugged within eyesight of the location," according to Laszlo.

Not mincing words, Waites remembers the conclave shoot as "a fucking nightmare"—speaking more for others than for himself. "It must have been brutal for Walter and the crew, because it was a lot of people. And Bobbie Mannix had to dress all these guys, some of whom were like, 'I'm not staying here.' So they would be in one shot and not in another. It went so long; I think it was supposed to take two days and it took six. That is very high pressure on a director, because the clock is ticking, the money is being watched by some bean counter, and they don't like it. Yet Walter remained rather calm under the circumstances, considering he was behind schedule and over budget.

"Now, a lot of movies get like that, but if you're, you know, Christopher Nolan or someone like that, they just let you do whatever you want. But Walter, it was his third picture, so they really put the screws to him, I'm sure. He claims that Frank Marshall and the other producers protected him from that as much as they could, but still, the studios will let you know when you're spending their money. But Walter's a tough guy; he's like a cowboy from the Wild West. You could see him walking down the street with two six-guns on either side of his hips, ready to have a drink and shoot it out with the next guy that crossed him."

At the same time, Mannix also has positive words for Hill's collaborative nature. "What's great about Walter is that when he hires a person to do costume design or production design or cinematography, he allows that person to do their job—that's why he hired you to begin with. I think he's the greatest, because he lets you have full rein to create and develop your own skill. He still says yes or no, but he lets you do the job he hired you for."

After Cyrus is shot, stunt coordinator Craig Baxley convinced Hill to let him stage a fall of about 15 feet—and had to perform it himself. "There were only two [black] stunt guys in New York at the time and neither one of them wanted to do it," Baxley told Ducker. "I came out with Afro Sheen in my hair and black skin with my blue eyes. I thought I would get killed. After I did the fall I got mobbed. They picked me up on their hands and were cheering."

The killing of Cyrus sparks a riot, the staging of which was left to Sosna to figure out. "Walter said, 'I want a riot.' I said, 'Well, what do you want to see?' He said, 'I'll put the camera here and look this way. I don't know—mix them up.' And he walked away." Sosna pauses before continuing, "So I had all these people who had never been in a movie before, they're tired, they don't know what to do, and I've got to make a riot. The great danger is, if I just take half on the left and half on the right and say, 'Run into each other,' I'll have dead bodies and a disaster."

His solution was to have three groups of gang members placed in concentric circles running in opposite directions around the camera. "I took the first 30 guys and put them in a line in front of me, facing left to right, then I took the next 30 guys and put them in a line behind the first line but had them facing right to left, and then a third line left to right behind those guys." Sosna then instructed them to run circles around the camera, "so what you see are the first and third groups going left to right, and the middle group going right to left, but in the size of the shot, you can't pick that out." He pauses again. "*I* could, because I staged it, but when you see it for 10 seconds and there's a cut to stunt guys falling and so on, it looks real."

It certainly looked real enough to Pauline Kael, who singled this sequence out in her *New Yorker* review: "[Hill's] staging of the park assembly and then its disintegration into a riot, with the gangs swarming in all directions, is reminiscent of the Babylonian scenes of D.W. Griffith's *Intolerance*." Decades later, Sosna hasn't forgotten her misattribution, which is common and just part of working behind the scenes in show business. "She gave the credit to Walter Hill, who just said, 'Mix them up.' It's like the stuntmen who always say, 'Yes, Tom Cruise does everything, I just eat a lot of hamburgers at lunch.' It's all an illusion. It's all fake. That's the whole idea—we're in the 'fake' business."

When taking part in a massive and chaotic sequence such as this, Garfield points out, "As an actor, you learn to really be careful, and to adjust everything you do, in regard to safety being the primary concern. And there were a lot of people on the set ensuring that there was safety. A simple thing like—and I remember because it was part of my bit—jumping over a railing on a stairway that might have only been a couple of feet off the ground was done by a stuntperson. They didn't want anybody to get hurt. And when the big crowd started moving around, everybody was very mindful of each other. You had to be, otherwise it would be extremely dangerous. And they choreographed it: 'Everybody in this line run to the right, everybody in this line run to the left,' so we knew exactly what we were doing."

Another actor in this scene who knew exactly what he was doing was Robert Townsend, years before he famously maxed out multiple credit cards to complete his indie comedy *Hollywood Shuffle* (1987). Like everyone else playing a gang member at the conclave, Townsend was directed to panic and flee the area as a reaction to Cyrus' killing, but since he was dressed in the uniform of a Gramercy Riff, he decided it would be more sensible to go check on the condition of his fallen leader. When "Action" was called, instead of running around the camera as Sosna had instructed, Townsend went over and knelt beside Cyrus' prone form—and found out later Hill had noticed this and restaged the shot to highlight his act of allegiance.

"In that moment, I, this little young actor in the middle of 700 people, had affected the scene," Townsend told IndieWire's Jim Hemphill. "After that, every time I walked on set, even though I was an extra I walked on the set like I was a director. 'What are we shooting today? What's the first shot?' And that's when I started to learn about directing in a weird, crazy way." Townsend was later cast in a featured role in *Streets of Fire*.

Actor-filmmaker Robert Townsend on the set of his 1991 film *The Five Heartbeats*.

It was during the filming of the conclave and the riot that Copeland rose from extra to stuntman, having initially been hired simply to help fill in the crowd. "Sylvia Fay was doing all the background casting, and I went in for that, and there were hundreds of people there," he says of his entrée into the *Warriors* world. "I was wearing a shirt from the production of a movie called *Stunts*. I wasn't part of that film, but a buddy of mine was working at New Line Cinema, and he invited me up to the office to watch it. There were boxes there filled with these shirts that said, '*Stunts*: To Heck With Dialogue, Let's Wreck Something.' Of course, I got a couple of those, and I wore them when I went to the interviews, and lo and behold, I fell in with a crowd of guys who were also interested in doing stuntwork."

Copeland recalls one specific requirement for playing a gang member in *The Warriors*: "I had a mustache at the time, maybe a little goatee, and they asked me if I would shave it for the film. I said, 'Well, how many days am I going to be working?' 'We don't know, but the director says no one can have facial hair.' So I said, 'Sure, OK, I'll shave it.' And the next thing I know, I'm getting called in for work. I was a fight expert at the time; I was very into martial arts, Bruce Lee, all of the fighting forms, and I brought nunchucks with me to the set. If you remember, in the film no one was allowed to have weapons at the conclave. But I had my nunchucks, and nobody stopped me, and I'm right on the front line as an Electric Eliminator with the nunchucks on my shoulder."

During breaks in filming, Copeland and some of the other extras would practice martial arts moves, and Baxley noticed the nunchucks, which Copeland had made himself from hickory hammer handles and chains purchased in Chinatown. "He came over and said, 'Hey, can I use those in the film?' I said, 'Sure, all right, but what about me?' He said, 'Well, I'll see what I can do.' So he gave me a bit in the riot where I jump up on a scaffold when the police are coming, and then I jump down. I did that well, and then he gave me another scene where I'm fighting with one of the police officers who comes in in riot gear. They didn't really tell us what to do, but these guys had real billy clubs, and they were whacking the daylights out of us. So I started choreographing the scene, and Baxley saw me do this and said, 'I'd have to train a guy for five years to do what you just did there in 10 minutes. You should be a stuntman.'

"So then I did another fight scene with an actor who I became friends with, Eddie Earl Hatch, and Craig gave me a stair fall, and that was the beginning of my work on *The Warriors*. I worked all summer on the movie; a lot of it was what they call ND stunts, nondescript stunts." But his most pivotal gag in the film was yet to come...

Following the bedlam in the park, the Warriors manage to slip away to a nearby graveyard, which in fact was Evergreen Cemetery in Brooklyn's Cypress Hills section. As Laszlo told *Filmmaker Monthly*'s Chuck Austin, he had to give the site an atypical mood. "The cemetery does not function in *The Warriors* as it would in your typical horror film as the place where the audience is supposed to feel the greatest fear for its characters. In this picture the cemetery is where the gang takes refuge...and it had to have the feeling of escape and safety, as if it were the most wonderful place in the world to be at midnight."

Riverside Park was also the site of another key setpiece: the Warriors' dustup with the Baseball Furies. For this and other brawls, Hill insisted

Remar's Ajax faces off with a Baseball Fury in Riverside Park.

that the actors do their own fighting, so Baxley gave the cast a crash course in screen fisticuffs. For his initial confrontation with one of the Furies, Remar improvised Ajax's line, "I'll shove that bat up your ass and turn you into a popsicle"—appropriate to his homophobic (as well as misogynistic) character, whose insult of choice is "faggot."

Despite their brief training, the cast did take the occasional hit during the *Warriors* shoot. "I got punched for real by Dorsey Wright," Weiss says. "I jumped into the fray, and the original punch was a roundhouse, and then they changed it, and I got it right in the face and fell down. Frank Marshall said, 'We need a replacement for Cropsey!' and I jumped right up and said, 'What, are you kidding me?' I couldn't believe it had happened, but they got it on film, so that was that.

"I also broke my finger on *The Warriors*, but not during filming," he adds. "If you watch me when I'm driving at the end of the movie, there's black tape over two of my fingers. I was off the set for a week, and I learned my lesson: You can't play sports on your off time. I was playing touch football, and this guy said, 'Think fast!' and I didn't, and I broke two fingers. They put a splint on them, but when I went back to the movie, I took the splint off and put the tape on them."

Back in the '70s, the New York subways were synonymous with crime and danger, but as the Warriors battle their way south through Manhattan, the underground trains become a vital lifeline, and the city's transit system collectively became a key location. "The Transit Authority had a few reservations about the screenplay," Marshall told *Film Bulletin* in an interview quoted in the press notes, "however they eventually gave us invaluable cooperation, allowing us to use real subway stations, including the one at 96th Street [though the Warriors exit at the relabeled 72nd Street station] and the huge Union Square complex. They also allowed us to film during entire nights, uninterrupted, on moving trains, which hadn't been done before." One of the cast added, "I've lived in New York all my life, and I'd never been on a subway as much as I was for this movie."

The crew also filmed in disused portions of the Hoyt-Schermerhorn station, a popular shooting site for features ranging from *The Taking of Pel-*

ham One Two Three (1974), *The Wiz* (1978) and *Teenage Mutant Ninja Turtles* (1990) to the horror cheapie *Devil's Express*, a.k.a. *Gang Wars* (1976). The only set that was constructed (at Astoria Studios in Queens, now known as Kaufman Astoria Studios) was the Union Square station men's room where the Warriors battle the Punks, since no actual bathroom could be found that was large enough to accommodate this action.

"What really pissed me off was that I was looking for that bathroom [location] for weeks, without success, and I finally found one in a high school on the Upper West Side," says Ryder. "I took a whole bunch of Polaroids and went to Walter on the set and said, 'Check this out! I found it!' He looked at me and said, 'Nah, I don't like it.' All along, he knew he wanted that bathroom built. Paramount didn't want to pay for it, but he just insisted on it. Finally, they built it out in Queens. It had flyaway walls

The Warriors and The Punks do battle on the movie's only constructed set.

and all that shit that made it a *lot* easier to shoot in. You have total control. You can see why directors would want to do that."

But first, those "flyaway" walls had to pass Hill's inspection. According to Sosna, "We went and looked at the set, and Walter said, 'Show me how this works.' So the stunt guys started throwing each other into the walls, and Walter said, 'I can see the wall move.' It was a studio wall that was braced, but obviously it wasn't braced well enough. Walter said, 'We can't shoot this until it's braced better, so we can throw people against it and it doesn't wiggle.' So we went and shot something else the next day while a couple of construction guys worked on it, and then we came back when the set was declared 'ready to go.' "

Throughout the shoot, Laszlo, making the first of three collaborations with Hill—it was followed by *Southern Comfort* (1981) and *Streets of Fire*—faced the challenge of giving the characters and their surroundings the proper illumination while remaining faithful to the way New York streets really look at night. The conclave sequence posed particular hurdles, as the area in which it was shot was relatively small and had to appear much more expansive, as well as accommodate the necessary equipment and non-professional extras, who were not trained in performing for the camera. "The lighting also caused problems because we had to have generators here and there," Laszlo recalled to Austin, "but certain other areas had to be dark so you could see the headlights of the police cars pulling up and the police truck with its search light blinding people."

One solution to a practical concern wound up becoming a key part of *The Warriors'* vibrant veneer, its streets glistening with reflected lights and colors. As Laszlo explained to Austin, "...we created a thunderstorm early in the story just to make sure that should it rain while we were shooting, we wouldn't be closed down because everything would be wet whereas it was dry in the previous cut... Of course what happens with wet pavements is that while they give you nice reflections and neons and so on, they also give you a tremendous amount of kicks and harshness. But we wanted that harshness."

"I remember Andy Laszlo setting up these fantastic shots that really gave an actor room to play," Waites praises. "He wet down the streets before every shot, so they glimmered and shimmered in the light. He painted beautiful pictures that Walter could work within. They had a very symbiotic relationship, the two of them. They communicated well, and understood one another, and I think the picture has a visual quality unlike anything I've ever seen, except for maybe *A Clockwork Orange*."

Not surprisingly, the production attracted the attention of plenty of spectators, who would hang out to watch the shooting late into the night, even with temperatures falling into the 50s. However, some were there only to cause disruptions. "They'd turn up their boomboxes," says Ryder. "By that point I was in front of the cameras so I didn't have to deal with that shit, but there were different ways of paying them off, promising them they could be in the movie—whatever if they'd just shut the fuck up. That's really common in movies, where you have looky-loos and people making trouble. It's a huge hassle when you're shooting on location and having to deal with that stuff."

Occasionally, though, locals not in the know would get scared by the film's *faux* gangs. One night, a group of the actors playing the fearsome-looking, skinheaded Turnbull A.C.'s went to grab some food at a burger restaurant, and the place emptied out within seconds. Even after the patrons were assured that this was not an actual gang incursion, they were hesitant about coming back in.

Then there were the real-life gangs to deal with. As Marshall told *The Village Voice*'s Connor, "There were city permits that you had to have to shoot...but then there was the cash you had to have on hand to spread around to keep everybody happy. It was all part of getting permission to be in the neighborhoods. The different territories were very much like in the movie." A contact within the NYPD helped Marshall keep peace with the local toughs: "Our gang advisor would tell us what gang was part of what neighborhood, whether it was a dangerous gang or not, and we tried to go where the friendly gangs were."

One night in a burned-out part of the Bronx, Beck remembers, the cash didn't find its way into the right hands. "The powers in the real gang world had not been paid off in this particular locale," he told Ducker. "So out of these derelict buildings, on the second and third floors all these faces of people, who we learned later were gang guys...just started yelling and screaming and making so much noise that we couldn't shoot there."

Ryder remembers a few instances where real gang members were hanging around and causing problems, but by then the production had found a way to deal with them. "We had a couple of security guys who were moonlighting NYPD—I think they might've been detectives—but they were mean motherfuckers," he reveals. "They were big and they wore these black, kind of long raincoats. When there was a problem, they would just go take care of it. It was one of those things where everyone in production would be like, 'Don't ask, don't tell how they handled that,' because they'd rough people up and make them go away."

Other gang members in Harlem objected to the fact that none of their own had been cast in the film, and issued death threats against Hill, Gordon and Marshall, who required police protection as a result. "We tried not to publicize the shooting too much," Marshall remarked in the production notes, "attempting to keep a low profile, for reasons of street control. But we did unavoidably run into some real gang problems... We learned very quickly that you don't fool around with those guys." Gordon added, "We had some run-ins with gangs during the summer, but the fact that nothing really serious happened was, I think, due to the fact that we laid low."

Still, even though these encounters left the people unscathed, there were casualties: One set was attacked during a lunch break, resulting in thousands of dollars' worth of damage to equipment. These sorts of problems continued throughout the shoot: "We were shooting in the Bronx up in the projects and they were tossing bricks off at the crew," Baxley says, and Weiss recalled to Ducker that life imitated art and interfered with their progress: "My scene at Avenue A we had to cancel filming. There was a double homicide up the block." On another night, the filming of the

Warriors' altercation with the Orphans was interrupted by the lights and sirens of an actual vehicle pursuit between police and a robbery suspect.

As if the problems with people outside the production weren't difficult enough, a contentious situation arose between Hill and Waites as well. The fledgling actor was dissatisfied both with the production conditions—he complained to the Screen Actors Guild about all eight Warriors actors being forced to share one trailer, resulting in a second one being added—and because his role wasn't turning out as he envisioned. "I was being annoying, and overly questioning," he admits. "I guess I just got afraid. The movie we had talked about making and the one we were actually making just seemed to be two different things, and I was like, whoa, there's so much violence. I thought this was going to be a love story about a guy and a girl and how their love rises above it, and 'Yeah, yeah, that's what we're going to do.' And then it just seemed like the violence became much more important.

"I guess I resented that and started questioning Walter about it," Waites continues, "which was really none of my business. Of course, you do have

Alas, Mercy and the Fox's romance was not to be.

a right to participate to a certain extent, but you should go through proper channels, like your agent or whatever, and say, 'I have concerns. Can we make time to discuss them?' But instead, I was bothering him on the set, and I just drove him crazy. And let it be a lesson to whoever's reading this: Don't piss off the director. Even if you don't like him, or even if he doesn't like you, you focus on the work. Do the job you were hired to do. Keep your mouth shut and listen. I was just not doing that."

Weiss notes that a hint of the impending trouble occurred when the cast got together for a table read of the *Warriors* script. "Everybody was there—Walter, Frank Marshall, everybody. We were reading the whole movie, and it was intense, it was going well, and then all of a sudden, Tom Waites, in the middle of it, said, 'Excuse me, do we have room for improvisation?' And there was dead silence. We were all really into it, and I knew from other situations that this was not cool. I mean, this didn't count, no one was filming it, but we were all into the flow, and he wanted to interrupt that."

The tension came to a head while filming a scene in which police chase the Warriors through the Hoyt-Schermerhorn station. It was at this point that Hill and the producers set in motion their plan to kill off the Fox character and rid themselves of Waites, but they needed to do it in a stealth manner that wouldn't telegraph to the actor that he was about to be fired. The deception required Sosna to keep him on "the board" in name only for scenes he would no longer be around to shoot. " 'The board' is a big piece of cardboard with vertical strips, each strip representing a scene," Sosna explains. "The actors are in numbered slots on there. Beck was one, Waites was two, Van Valkenburgh might've been three..." Sosna and Marshall worked out a secret code using dots to differentiate between the scenes they needed Waites for and the ones he'd never appear in, while concealing from the actor a whole new scene that wasn't in the script (but still had to be on the board) in which his character would be killed. It was all done to keep Waites from knowing that this was going to be his last night on the film.

"So we did the scene: Some guy punches him, and we see him fall to the ground. Then we said, 'OK, Tom, you're wrapped for the day. Everything else is without you. You can go home.' 'Thanks! See you tomorrow!' No you won't, but we won't tell you that now."

Today, Waites rues the fact that he was never given a warning that his behavior was going to lead to his dismissal. "That's the one regret I have. I wish Walter would have taken me aside and said, 'Look, motherfucker, you back off of me! Leave me the fuck alone, quit talking to me unless you have to, or I'm going to fire your ass.' I would have been like, 'Yes, sir! I'm sorry, sir.' But I didn't get a warning, I just got dropped."

Instead, Waites got the fateful call from his agent, Jeff Hunter, while at his girlfriend's house in Upper Bucks County, PA. "It was a Saturday, and we were waiting to hear what our call times would be for Monday. The phone rang and they said, 'It's your agent'—and he would normally not call Janet's house, so I knew something was up. I answered the phone, and he said, 'They don't want you back.' 'What are you talking about? I just signed a three-picture deal with Paramount.' As you can imagine, my heart dropped into my stomach, and I felt physically ill, because I knew it was my fault. I knew there was no one to blame except myself. Walter's been generous enough to allow me to try to make half-assed amends, and I think he has forgiven me for it. The hard part was forgiving myself, because this could have been a great opportunity for my career. It was a very painful experience for me, and I hope that I tried to make the best use of it as possible."

Although, as noted above, his *Warriors* co-star Remar wound up being dismissed from *Aliens* early in its shoot several years later, Waites has never compared notes or commiserated with Remar about the incidents. "I heard about it, of course, and he clearly bounced back from that. It didn't stop him, and he went on to have a terrific and still is having a terrific career. You know, a lot of great actors have been fired; I'm not saying I'm a great actor, just that it's happened to a lot of them. It sort of comes with the territory."

Baxley recalls that Hill insisted he come up with a way to kill off the Fox quickly. The solution was to dress a double in Waites' costume and have one of the cops throw the Fox onto the tracks, in front of an oncoming train. That's where Copeland came in. He recalls that he had gone to see the Burt Reynolds stuntman movie *Hooper*, "and that night, I got a phone call from [the *Warriors*] production that they wanted me on the set. I didn't know what for. These were the days before cell phones, and I was such a poor actor at the time, a poor stuntman, I couldn't even afford a telephone. So it was on my answering service, and I called up production the next day and they said, 'Come down to the set.'

"They were filming at Hoyt-Schermerhorn," he continues, "and it was the scene where the Fox gets thrown in front of the subway train. So I was hired to do this fight and then fall down onto the tracks. They evidently used a grip, I believe, to do the run down the platform the night before, when I didn't get the message and make it to the set. Then they used me to do the actual struggle where the policeman comes out from behind the post in the subway, tackles me, and we roll around on the platform. I had no padding, and my arms were getting all skinned up, but I was handy and I had been doing a lot of boxing at Gleason's Gym at the time, where I wasn't getting paid anything. So this was great, because here I was getting paid, and I got thrown in front of the subway train, which was a big event."

As *The Warriors* was shot in sequence, it was easy to write the Fox out of the rest of the story with no necessity for reshoots, and Swan, who was originally intended to be captured by a homosexual gang called the Dingos (see Chapter Three), took over the lead and the relationship with Mercy. Waites took his name off the movie, and quickly rebounded: Three weeks after his dismissal, he won a key role opposite Al Pacino in *...and justice for all.* (1979). He also portrayed Windows in John Carpenter's *The Thing* (1982) and landed a number of high-profile stage gigs.

Conversely, a couple of actors found that their ill-fated roles on the page were given a new lease on life as filming progressed. "In the original script," Michos reveals in the notes, "the guy I portray, Vermin, gets killed, but Walter liked what I was doing with the part and changed things around so that I get to stay until the end of the picture. I owe my life to Walter Hill!" Similarly, Harris told Ducker, "At one point my character [Cochise] was supposed to get killed and dumped into the Hudson River. I end up in a park by myself and I get caught by these guys [the Baseball Furies]. It came down from the studio that Cochise is not going to die."

By the time *The Warriors* got to its climactic daytime scenes set at Coney Island, it was overbudget and nearly four weeks behind schedule. Part of the reason, Laszlo explained to Austin, was that the filmmakers often altered their schedule on the spot: "...many times we were in situations where it would become obvious that, after our 'lunch' (which was served at midnight), the remaining time that night would probably not be enough to complete the sequence scheduled for that time period. So we would just abandon it. Immediately. And say, 'OK, let's do something else and

Originally intended to die at the Furies' hands, Cochise (David Harris) lived to fight another gang.

we'll start with that other part first thing tomorrow.' The attitude was never one of 'Let's get it in the can because it was scheduled for today and come hell and high water we're going to get it over with.' There was never any rush."

Despite all the issues involved in the prior night shoots, Laszlo says that the final moments on the Coney Island beach were among the most difficult, dealing with crashing waves and fading sunlight. In addition, this area was the stamping grounds of an actual gang called the Homicides, who were agreeable to the cast and crew using their turf but would not tolerate anyone wearing the colors of another gang, fictional or not. As a result, the actors all had to change clothes if they strayed anywhere outside the immediate filming area, even to go to lunch.

A creative issue that arose at the beginning of this sequence involved the arrival of Luther and his Rogues; Hill knew Luther needed a strong entrance, but wasn't sure what that should be. He asked Kelly to come up

Kelly, improvising one of *The Warriors* classic moments.

with something, and the actor's initial idea literally didn't fly. "We improvised that scene; there was no rehearsal," Weiss reveals. "We got in the car, and the first take was David saying, 'Warriors, come out to play!' and in the middle of that, I said, 'We're gonna get you, Warriors!' But the rhythm with him alone was better. Then I saw David pick up two dead pigeons, put them in a bag, go up to Walter and show that to him, and Walter said, 'No, we're not doing that.' " Instead, Kelly collected a few small-serving beer bottles he found strewn around the area, clicked them together, and came up with the singsong delivery inspired by a strange character who had harassed him in his neighborhood. Today, "Warriors! Come out to play-ay!" remains the movie's best-remembered, most-repeated line.

Weiss recalls another issue that cropped up in Coney when the Rogues' hearse pulls in behind the Warriors. "When I read the script, it said, 'Cropsey starts the car,' " he explains. "I didn't know how to drive, so I was like, 'I gotta take driver's education'—and I failed the test with a 48!

The danger was just a little bit real when the Rogues' hearse moved in on the Warriors.

"So then we were in Coney Island, I had all the guys in the car with me, and I was driving it slowly. Then we brought it back; I didn't back the car up, somebody else did. Walter said, 'Cropsey, I need you to go faster!' And I wish we had stills of the take where I was going faster; they're walking tough through Coney Island, and you had to see Michael Beck and all of them go like, 'Oh my God!' So they brought the car back again, and Walter said, 'Cropsey, get out of the car,' but not in a mean way. I was mad at myself over this, but Walter said, 'I hired you as an actor, not a driver. We'll figure that out later.' "

The determination that *The Warriors* be the first gang film into theaters (several others were also in the works; see Chapter Four) led Paramount to set up three cutting rooms to get the picture into shape quickly. David Holden, the only editor to get upfront credit, began his work right after production started, and told The Warriors Movie Site, "I had a crushing amount of footage to deal with; we nicknamed Walter Hill 'the blanket' because he covered *everything*. After a while cutting in NYC, Freeman Davies came from LA to help me out, then Billy Weber joined the two of us when we moved back to LA... We had a rough cut ready three days after shooting ended."

The actors, who hadn't been allowed to attend dailies, got their first look at *The Warriors* when they were invited to a screening at the Gulf + Western Building. Because no one warned them beforehand that what they were about to watch was a rough cut and therefore unfinished, most of their reactions were resoundingly negative. Michos recalls, "We all walked out of there so upset—'This is gonna be the most awful film ever seen'—and Larry Gordon got wind of that. I remember him saying to Walter or Frank Marshall, 'I told you we should've never let these guys see it like this! It isn't done! I knew it—I knew you shouldn't have let them see it!' "

Beck told Talbot, "I remember the conversations... '*That's what it's gonna look like?!*' And Walter was saying, '*That's not what it's gonna look like.*' For most of us, it was the first time we'd seen a rough cut. I was still green enough to think, 'Well, I guess things can be fixed a little bit.' Most of us weren't able to say, '*Oh, it's gonna be color corrected.*' "

The final touch was the score by Barry DeVorzon, a former record producer and songwriter whose greatest screen success to that point had been with the anti-animal-violence drama *Bless the Beasts and Children* (1971). He got an Oscar nomination for the title song (performed by The Carpenters) and adapted one of his pieces from the soundtrack into 'Nadia's Theme' for the soap opera *The Young and the Restless*, winding up with a Top 10 hit. As opposed to those benign tracks, DeVorzon was inspired to give *The Warriors* an aggressive, all-rock soundtrack making use of synthesizers, which were then just starting to make their mark in the pop/rock/disco scene as well as on movie screens. German electronica artists Tangerine Dream had nabbed their first major film assignment on *Sorcerer* (1977), and Giorgio Moroder won a Best Original Score Oscar for his pulsing synth beats in *Midnight Express* (1978).

"An orchestral score just didn't seem to make any sense for this picture," DeVorzon told *Village Voice* interviewer Dan Hyman. "Plus, I was dying to try out bringing in some contemporary sounds." One of his inspirations on *The Warriors* resulted in another popular song. He was friends with The Eagles' Joe Walsh and corralled Walsh to co-write and sing the end-credits tune "In the City," which also appeared on the Eagles' 1979 album *The Long Run*; that record spent eight weeks at the top of the *Billboard* charts, selling over eight million copies. (Weiss recalls that in the rough cut, the movie's closing moments were temp-tracked with "Promised Land" by Bruce Springsteen, who at the time was resistant to allowing his songs to be used in movies.)

The Warriors had a little more of DeVorzon's work running through it than the composer and Hill initially intended, as the two hadn't wanted any music playing during the fight with the Baseball Furies. They felt the action spoke for itself, but Gordon (who had previously employed DeVorzon on 1973's *Dillinger*, 1977's *Rolling Thunder* and Hill's *Hard Times*) felt

it needed DeVorzon's accompaniment. Later, on the DVD, DeVorzon conceded that Gordon was right: "Without music, the scene is much more violent. With music, it in some way reminds the viewer, this is just a game."

The Warriors went through a few other significant changes on its way to release. The film originally opened with daytime scenes in which Cleon talks with his girlfriend (played by Pamela Poitier), and then rallies the gang for the trip uptown to the conclave. Holden believed that starting the story in the sunlight would work against the overall mood, and so these scenes were excised; to replace them, Hill shot brief scenes of the characters discussing the conclave on the Coney Island platform, and intercut them with shots of hurtling subway trains and the Warriors and other gangs making their way uptown.

A more significant loss was a prologue and other scenes introducing and explicating the connections between *The Warriors* and *Anabasis*, for which Hill wanted none other than Orson Welles to provide the narration. (Marshall and Canton had worked with the legendary actor on his then-unfinished final directorial effort *The Other Side of the Wind*, which was finally released in 2018.) Paramount wouldn't pick up the tab for Welles' services, nor would they ultimately go for Hill's concept of comic-art panels in the intro and interstitial bits appearing throughout the film.

"I didn't think the film would work without the reference to Greek history," Hill told DGA interviewer Robert Markowitz. "I thought you should say a bit of that. You also had to say this took place in the near future, science fiction a bit. And third that it was lurid and comic-book. The best way to deal with it was to use comics to introduce the approach to character and narrative. The studio had agreed to this approach, in post we did not agree."

In addition, Hill told Ducker, "I had a very simple thing at the beginning of the movie which [Paramount] wouldn't let me do which was a legend that said, 'Some time in the future.' The great minds at the studio thought that was too much like *Star Wars*. I thought the movie was close to being incomprehensible without that because it always seemed to me to be a science fiction movie."

And then there were the many changes between Hill's screenplay and the final feature, as detailed in our next chapter...

3 *The Warriors:* Alternative Visions

If the relationship between Walter Hill and actor Thomas G. Waites hadn't deteriorated as quickly and thoroughly as it did, *The Warriors* would have been a very different film from the one that opened in 600-plus theaters on February 9, 1979. A revised screenplay by Hill dated June 20th, 1978—less than a week before the first day of filming—provides a fascinating look at the story Hill originally intended to tell. It also presents an airtight argument for filming the gang's A-to-B-to-C journey from Coney Island to the Bronx and back entirely in sequence.

Like many of Hill's screenplays, this draft of *The Warriors* starts with a preamble of several pages that establishes the key players as well as the tone of the story. The first two pages consist of a brief description of each of the nine delegates chosen to represent the Warriors at Cyrus' upcoming conclave in the Bronx, beginning with Cleon (the leader of the gang, blessed with "a tightly controlled intensity") and ending with Ajax ("cantankerous at best" with "a natural inclination for mixing violence and sex").

There are several interesting takeaways from this section, the first one being that Rembrandt is singled out as the Fox's "best friend." Additionally, we learn that among the other gang members, Ajax most dislikes the Fox, although "Swan is a close second." In the finished film, there's no indication that Ajax feels more animosity toward the Fox than any other Warrior, and, except for one look between them during the graveyard scene, nothing to suggest that the Fox and Rembrandt are especially close. The only other point worth noting is that Snowball "never speaks," a character trait that—like the dichotomy between the Fox and other gang members—

The Warriors assemble in front of their building-spanning tag (not seen in the film).

must have been refigured once it became apparent that Waites would be exiting the project much earlier than planned.

The third page contains the following description of the events depicted in Xenophon's *Anabasis*...

> *In the Fourth Century before Christ,*
> *a mercenary army of Greek soldiers*
> *found themselves stranded in the*
> *middle of the Persian Empire.*
> *One thousand miles from the sea.*
> *One thousand miles from safety.*

Enemy troops around them on every
quarter.
This is a story of that army's forced march.
This is a story of courage.
This is a story of War.

This intro is similar to the one Hill added to the beginning of his Ultimate Director's Cut in 2005, which appears under a drawing that depicts the Battle of Cunaxa in 401 B.C.:

Over two millenniums ago,
an army of Greek soldiers
found themselves isolated in the
middle of the Persian Empire.
One thousand miles from safety.
One thousand miles from the sea.
One thousand miles
with enemies on all sides.
Theirs was a story of a
desperate forced march.
Theirs was a story of courage.
This too is a story of courage.

However, the "Sometime in the future..." that is superimposed over the opening shot of the Wonder Wheel in the Ultimate Director's Cut is nowhere to be found in the screenplay, which leads one to question Hill's assertion in 2005 that he had originally intended the film to begin with this note. In fact, there is nothing else in the screenplay that would make anyone believe this story takes place in the future, though Hill told *Millimeter* magazine's Mark Patrick Carducci during the shoot, "I see *The Warriors* as a fantasy. I want the time to be understood as ten or fifteen years into the future; not that it's science fiction, not at all....Future fiction." (Meanwhile, a poster for the Goldie Hawn-Chevy Chase comedy *Foul Play* that is clearly visible in one of the subway stations sets the story firmly in the summer of 1978.)

The last two pages of the preamble consist of a montage titled "Gangs of New York on the Move..." that is basically the footage shown during the opening credits of various gangs leaving their turf and boarding Bronx-bound subway trains, among them a black gang from the Lower East Side (the Boppers), an Irish gang from Staten Island (the Gerrards), and an Italian gang from Queens (the Knockdowns), along with the High-Hats from Roosevelt Island, the Boyle Avenue Runners from Astoria, the Gladiators from Canarsie, the Howitzers from Bedford-Stuyvesant, and the Electric Eliminators from Harlem.

The story begins on the next page. We fade in on a graffiti-covered building near the Coney Island boardwalk, where Rembrandt is creating art on the wall with a spray-paint can. It is immediately obvious that the

Coney Island's Wonder Wheel, a landmark now inextricably linked to *The Warriors.*

name "Rembrandt" has been glued over another name, a replacement that appears on every page that is either undated or revised prior to June 19, 1978. An oversight on page 62 reveals the character's original name to be Plato, and on page 98 "Plato" has been crossed out with a pen and "REM" written underneath.

On the beach, Ajax is working out on a pair of rings. The Fox begins taunting him: "Oooo. Big Man. Look at all those muscles." Ajax calls him a "faggot" and warns him to watch his mouth. The Fox responds with "Lighten up, big boy, save yourself for the girlies." This exchange establishes a homoerotic tension between the two gang members while also foreshadowing the scene in Riverside Park when Ajax accosts and is arrested by the undercover policewoman ("Look at those muscles," she says. "Bet the girlies like all those muscles...").

Nearby, Swan displays his blade-throwing prowess by catching windblown paper scraps with a Bowie knife. The Fox reminds him that Cyrus has called a one-day truce for the conclave in the Bronx: "No guns, no blades, no weapons for anybody." Swan is edgy, not only because he can't bring his knife—as a Warrior, he's never been without it—but because Ajax "ain't much of a soldier if things go bad."

Back on the boardwalk, Cleon has a conversation with Lincoln, the girlfriend he has just gotten back together with after a recent dalliance. She is worried that Cleon will get "messed up with something heavy way off in the Bronx," a part of the city he's never been to, and she wants him to stay behind. "I like everything just the way it is," she tells him.

Later, Cleon meets with the eight soldiers he has chosen (from "a street family of 120") to accompany him on the expedition to the Bronx. Swan is "War Chief," second in command to Cleon. Snowball is "the music man," which means he carries a boombox radio. Ajax, Cochise and Cowboy are "soldiers in the middle, heavy muscle." Vermin is "the bearer," entrusted with the subway tokens and travel money. Rembrandt is in charge of leaving the gang's mark in spray paint all along their journey ("Hit everything in sight," Cleon stresses. "I want people to know the Warriors was there.").

The Fox is "scout and memory man" because of his encyclopedic knowledge of every gang in the five boroughs. The nine delegates then depart for the D train, beginning their 30-mile journey north to Van Cortlandt Park in the Bronx.

All the scenes up to this point have been daytime exteriors. Once the decision was made to have the Warriors' journey take place entirely at night (as noted in Chapter Two), Hill brought back eight of the nine actors and shot selected lines of dialogue from these introductory scenes to use in the snappy opening-credits sequence. This is why the Fox doesn't appear in these short dialogue bits; once Waites was written out of the film, Snowball became a speaking role and the recipient of some of the Fox's lines.

However, when *The Warriors* made its network television debut on *The ABC Friday Night Movie* on February 25, 1983, devoted fans were surprised to see a different opening than the one they were accustomed to, as a couple of these deleted scenes were reinserted after the Paramount

Vermin, Cochise and Ajax share some lighter moments on the subway before things get very dark, in scenes added late in production.

Pictures logo: the bulk of Cleon's conversation with Lincoln (Pamela Poitier) and the entirety of Cleon's boardwalk pep talk, ending with the Warriors' departure for the subway while "Rumble" by Link Wray & His Ray Men blasts forth from Snowball's boombox. As redundant and awkward as these scenes are, they are not completely without interest. Lincoln's concern for Cleon seems genuine, and Poitier makes the most of what little screen time she has. Dorsey Wright's hair is shown briefly before Cleon puts on his leopard-skin keffiyeh.

As for the other Warriors, the one to watch is Terry Michos as Vermin, whose wide-eyed nervousness here is totally at odds with his performance in the rest of the film. "If you go back to the graveyard scene, you'll see even then I didn't know what I was doing with my character," Michos affirms. "I was trying to be tough, because I was a Warrior, but *all* of these guys were tough, and their characters were tough, and their lines were tough... 'Swan's war chief,' 'Lighten up, big boy,' 'We've got to stick together'—we were all sounding alike."

He decided then and there to make Vermin more distinctive from the others, and fine-tuned the character using an unlikely source for inspiration: the boy centaur, Newton, in *The Mighty Hercules*, a syndicated cartoon that premiered on television in 1963, when Michos was 9 years old. As the titular hero's sidekick, Newton provided comic relief with his habit of saying some of his lines twice. "He'd go, 'Herc! Herc!' or 'What are we going to do?! What are we going to do?!' and he'd talk in a little higher voice when he got nervous. So I decided, when Vermin gets nervous, I'm going to talk in a higher voice and I'm going to say things twice. 'Hurt me, hurt me.' 'We're going to get japped here, we're going to get japped.' "

To reach the Coney Island-Stillwell Avenue subway station, the Warriors must march through turf controlled by the Mongols, a gang that killed a member of the Warriors the year before. The Mongols honor the truce and let the Warriors pass, despite the barely contained hostility between both parties and Ajax's almost total lack of self-control. This scene is similar to the sequence in Sol Yurick's novel where the Coney Island Dominators must "bop" through the Colonial Lords' territory and Lunkface almost blows his stack with one of the more obnoxious Lords.

Comic book writer/artist Larry Hama revealed to interviewer Christopher Irving that he was one of the gang members in this scene, and that it was filmed in Tribeca rather than Coney Island. Since Hama also played one of the delegates from the Savage Huns in the conclave sequence, and can be glimpsed waiting on a subway platform with other Huns during the opening credits, he was either cast in two different Asian gangs or the Mongols were rewritten to be the Savage Huns once shooting began. Although a couple of production photos can be found on-line depicting the Warriors walking a gauntlet of Asian toughs on a cobblestone street in broad daylight, this scene has yet to surface in any television or home video releases of the film.

The network TV version also reinstates a brief scene, right after the opening credits, in which the Warriors wander the darkness of Van Cortlandt Park looking for the meeting place, albeit without the homophobic banter between Ajax and the Fox that appears in the screenplay (after being called a "faggot" again, the Fox repeats the word five times in falsetto). When the Warriors finally reach their destination, they find "a conclave of the principal gangs within the city" in "all their splendor, ornate finery and baroque appearance. Black, white, coffee-colored, Puerto Rican, Italian, Irish... More like an encampment of armies than a meeting."

What follows is an alphabetical list of the principal gangs in attendance:

The Alleycats, The Amsterdam All-Stars, The Black Hands, The Blackjacks, The Big Trains, The Boyle Avenue Runners, The Charlemagnes, The Colt 45's, The Dealers, The Delaney Rovers, The Dingos, The E Street Shufflers, The Easy Aces, The Electric Eliminators, The Eighth Avenue Apaches, The Fastballs, The Fifth Street Bombers, The Filmores, The Firetasters, The Five Points, The Gerrards, The Gladiators, The Go Hards, The Gun Hill Dancers, The Gramercy Riffs, The High Rollers, The Homeboys, The Hoplites, The Howitzers, The Huks, The Hurricanes, The Imps, The Jesters, The Jones Street Boys, The Judas Bunch, The Jupiters, The Knockdowns, The

Knuckles, The Locos, The Magicians, The Meatpackers, The Moonrunners, The Napoleons, The Nickel Steaks, The Nightriders, The Ninth Avenue Razors, The Panzers, The Phillies, The Plainsmen, The Queens Bridge Mutilators, The Red Hook Shooters, The Riffs, The Roadmasters, The Romans, The Runaways, The Saracens, The Saratogas, The Savage Huns, The Shanghai Sultans, The Southern Cross, The Speedwagons, The Stevedores, The Stilettos, The Stonebreakers, The Terriers, The Turks, The Turnbull A.C., The Vancourtland Rangers, The Whispers, The Xenophons, The Xylophones, The Yo-Yo's, The Youngbloods, The Zodiacs, and The Zulus.

As written, the scene at the conclave isn't much different from the finished film. The network TV version reinstates several lines from Cyrus' speech as they appear in the screenplay, but the only other difference worth noting is a short scene that hints at the violence to come. "How's our present for Cyrus," Luther asks his second in command, Cropsey, who is never referred to by name in the film (actor Joel Weiss is billed simply as a Rogue in the closing credits). "It works," Cropsey replies. "You sure," Luther presses him (question marks are nonexistent in Hill's writing). Smiling, Cropsey

Luther and Cropsey (Joel Weiss) just before the shooting sets off the action.

answers, "Real sure." "Cyrus is just going to love it," Luther says, smiling back. This exchange was wisely jettisoned in favor of the passing of the pistol from one Rogue hand to the next as the optimal way to introduce the Rogues and Luther.

After Cyrus is shot, the police raid the conclave. Cleon is accused by Luther and Cropsey of being the gunman and beaten to death by members of Cyrus' gang, the Gramercy Riffs. The other Warriors flee the park and reassemble in an adjacent cemetery, where the Fox informs the others that he saw who shot Cyrus: "Guy from the Rogues. South Bronx gang. Real punk....And he saw me." This line should not have been cut, since it explains how Swan and the others know who the Rogues are when they show up in Coney Island looking for the Warriors at the end of the film. In the screenplay, it's the Fox who first realizes that Cyrus' truce might be called off (Snowball gets this line in the finished film, in an awkward insert that was probably shot the same night as the opening-credits scenes), and it's also the Fox who suggests Union Square as the meeting place in case the Warriors get separated. Swan reiterates his idea a moment later, and that was kept because it leads into Ajax's attempted coup:

```
                    AJAX
          I only got one question.

     Pause.

                    AJAX
          Who named you leader.

     Suddenly no one is moving.

                    AJAX
          I got as much right to take over
          as you.

                  THE FOX
          It was Cleon's choice. Swan's
          War Chief.
```

AJAX

Right about now Cleon's most likely got a nightstick shoved halfway up his ass. **Fucking knives are the only reason you're up on anybody else. You're no leader without your blade and you ain't got one** ... Shit, I bet you can't even find the subway.

The **boldfaced section above**, another reference to Swan's superior skills with a knife, should also have remained in the film because it explains the precision throw that fells Luther at the climax. This is also the first of two instances in the film where a shot cuts away too late, just as a character—in this case Ajax—is about to speak, a clue that dialogue has been omitted.

There are other interesting differences in this scene. Rembrandt suggests that maybe they shouldn't try to get back to Coney Island right away, implying that they stay the night in the cemetery (something Hector wants to do in the novel), which leads to more friction and homophobic name-calling between Ajax and the Fox. Cochise asks about the radio, presumably so they can listen for a news update about the police activity at the conclave, but Snowball makes a thumbs-down sign. Since the two other scenes with the radio were already cut from the film, the decision to delete this was a no-brainer. (The radio's disappearance is only mentioned here for the benefit of the viewers. If the Warriors hear the word go out, they'll know that they've been blamed for Cyrus' death.)

The scene ends the same way as in the movie: Rembrandt undercuts the tension between Swan and Ajax by announcing that he can see elevated subway tracks in the distance. As the gang heads off in the direction of the train, Rembrandt marks the spot—spraying "W" on a gravestone—and then hurries off to join them.

At this point in the film, Masai (Edward Sewer)—the new leader of the Gramercy Riffs—sends word through the radio station DJ (Lynne Thigpen) to all the gangs in New York that "the real live bunch from Coney" is to be taken "alive if possible. If not, wasted..." This leads to a montage in which various gangs react to the message from the Riffs and set out to find the Warriors while a cover version of Martha & the Vandellas' "Nowhere to Run" (performed by Arnold McCuller) plays on the soundtrack.

In the screenplay, Masai—known as New Cyrus—and the DJ are introduced later (the DJ is never seen again after sending the word). Instead, the Warriors get caught in a rainstorm soon after leaving the cemetery to find the subway and must take cover under an awning, prompting this embarrassingly bad dialogue passage:

```
                 AJAX
Fucking lousy fucking train.

                VERMIN
This sucks.

               THE FOX
No shit.

                COWBOY
I'm beginning to think maybe
this ain't our night.

                 AJAX
Fucking A.

The rain continues to rip down.

                VERMIN
How long's this shit going to
keep up.

                COWBOY
Hey man, do I look like fucking
Channel Seven weatherman.
```

VERMIN

Shit no. You just look like a dumb fucker wearing a cowboy hat.

COWBOY

Hey man, fuck you.

VERMIN

You want to lay it down.

COWBOY

I'll lay you down, motherfucker.

The rain stops, and as the Warriors continue their hike to the subway station, Swan notices the gang mark for the Sports on a nearby building.

SWAN

Fox, give me a reading on the Sports.

THE FOX

Big outfit. Two hundred brothers. They got this one cat six-eight, call him Goliath, busts heads every night.

As expected, Ajax brands Goliath "chicken shit," the Fox takes the bait ("You'd be the first one to haul that ass of yours if you ran across him") and Ajax responds by calling the Fox a "faggot" again. Farther along, with still no subway station in sight ("Up here they can be a couple miles apart" the Fox tells a complaining Cochise), the Warriors suddenly hear a police siren approaching and take cover. Hiding in storefront doorways and the shadows of the elevated tracks overhead, they watch a police caravan pass by, escorting several buses packed with gang members who were arrested at Cyrus' conclave.

VERMIN

That's a few less for us to worry about.

COWBOY

I wonder if they had them Rogues on board.

THE FOX

That's one gang I'm glad I ain't in... I wouldn't want to be one of those mothers.

VERMIN

Just imagine if you had them Gramercy Riffs on your ass. Whewee...

AJAX

Probably just a bunch of chicken-shits.

Rembrandt looks after the police vans.

REMBRANDT

Wonder if they had Cleon in there.

Clips from this scene and the one where the Warriors run through the rain appear in the film as part of the "Nowhere to Run" montage. The screenplay cuts from Rembrandt's concern for Cleon to the Gramercy Riffs' clubhouse, where we learn Cleon is "dead as a fucking doornail" just before the New Cyrus sends the word and the DJ alerts the other gangs to look for the Warriors. Following the montage is the scene at the candy counter with the Rogues, which occurs later in the movie, after the track fire forces the Warriors off the subway.

The Warriors reach the subway station and spot the gang bus patrolling the street under the el tracks. In the screenplay, it's the Fox who IDs the gang as the Turnbull A.C.'s ("Those guys are killers....You got to be six foot tall just to get into that outfit"), while Snowball is the one who identifies them in the film.

The Turnbull A.C.'s prowl DP Andrew Laszlo's shimmering streets before taking off after the Warriors.

After the Warriors outrun the Turnbull A.C.'s and barely escape on the train, Ajax asks Rembrandt how many stops there are to Union Square, and Rembrandt starts to count on his fingers. "Come on, man, that's high math for Rembrandt," Cochise cracks, and Ajax asks if Rembrandt will need to count on his toes as well. The Fox tells Ajax to pound sand up his ass, and Ajax responds with his two favorite f-words and a "you" in between.

The update that Masai gets concerning the Turnbull A.C.'s ("They blew it"), which comes next in the film, is not in the screenplay. Instead, Hill cuts for comic effect from Vermin saying "We're home free" to a shot of firefighters dealing with a burning tenement adjacent to the subway trestle as the train lurches to a stop and smoke drifts across the tracks. A voice on a loudspeaker announces that, because of Fire Department orders, the train has been delayed indefinitely and buses are available to shuttle people the next station down the line. The Warriors watch the other passengers exit the train and converge on the stairwell leading down to the street.

COWBOY

This is fucking impossible.

VERMIN

What the shit are we going to do.
This sucks.

SWAN

Loudspeaker said take the buses,
so we're taking the buses.

COCHISE

Shit, this is really our night.

REMBRANDT

Why couldn't it rain now.

THE FOX

We just better worry about who
set the fire.

The **boldfaced section above** was filmed but not included in the movie (after Vermin's lines, the shot cuts away as Swan is starting to speak and goes right to Rembrandt saying "Why couldn't it rain now."). The Warriors get downstairs just as two crowded buses close their doors and pull away. Those remaining are told by an MTA employee that more buses will be coming along in a minute, which a few impatient passengers loudly translate as really meaning a half hour.

THE FOX

We ain't got a half hour.

Swan looks across the street.
The Fox stares in the opposite direction.

THE FOX

We've had it.

SWAN

I made them. One there,
two there.

The scene with the buses appears in the novel, and was definitely shot (David Sosna's first task as AD on the film was clearing the street and setting up this sequence), but like the gang's march through Mongols turf, it didn't make the final cut and hasn't been seen since. In its place is the scene with the Rogues at the candy counter, which occurs earlier in the screenplay. A visual "wipe" takes us from the counter to Swan and the Fox spotting the Orphans on the rooftops (the flashing lights of the fire trucks are still visible against the buildings in the background). Swan's decision to take the Fox along to assist in the parleying with the First Orphan causes the expected chafing among the Warriors:

SWAN

No matter what he says, nobody
lip off, nobody get hot. I'm
going to see what I can do.

AJAX

When did you turn into a fucking
diplomat.

VERMIN

Yeah, you ain't exactly the State
Department type.

THE FOX

It's better than sending assholes like you two over...

VERMIN

Maybe Ajax has got a point about you, Fox.

AJAX

Fucking A.

Swan looks down the street. Stares at the Orphan.

SWAN

Fox, you come with me.

AJAX

Why you taking that faggot.

SWAN

Because he's got a brain. He might know something useful.

THE FOX

Yeah, put a lid on it, Ape Man.

Swan and the Fox are almost successful with the parley. Admiring their vests, Mercy asks the name of their "family" and noticeably reacts when the Fox tells her they are members of the Warriors. "You guys are the big dudes," she says (a line that was cut from the film but is in the theatrical trailer). "That makes those vests real valuable."

When they refuse to give her one of their vests...

Mercy wheels on the First Orphan.

MERCY

You just going to let an army walk through here whenever they

```
        feel like it. How's that going
        to look...

    The point scores, but the First Orphan tries to
    shrug it off...

                    FIRST ORPHAN
        Get lost. You're just looking
        for a little action...

                       MERCY
        Yeah, and I'm gonna find it.
        Pretty soon the Stompers, the
        Masai, the Homeboys, the Meat-
        packers, the Easy Aces, every
        gang is just going to mambo
        right in.... Soldier right
        through... Some man you are.
```

There are two more minor differences in the scripted Orphans sequence vs. what appears in the final film. The first is that a dozen Orphans

Paul Greco's character, known as Sully in the screenplay, is billed simply as one of the "Orphans" in the end credits.

follow the Warriors for a few blocks, but then circle around to block their path to the subway entrance. The other difference is that after the Molotov cocktail is thrown and the car explodes, scattering the Orphans, Swan decides to take Mercy with them ("We may need her for a trade..."). The Fox then grabs her and says, "Come on, hot pants. You're the only hostage we got."

The two short scenes that come next in the film—Masai receiving the report that a "small-time clique" from outside the network "got wasted" in the Bronx by the Warriors, followed by the DJ announcing to all the Boppers that their "friends made it past one of the minor league teams"—are not in the screenplay. Instead, the story goes right from the Orphans to the scene with the Rogues at the gas station. In the film, a visual wipe brings us from there to the 96th Street subway station and the last time we see Waites as the Fox.

When the Warriors elude the police at 96th Street, the division of members is different in the screenplay: the Fox, instead of being thrown to his death, takes off with Mercy into the subway tunnel while Cowboy (not Cochise) catches a downtown train with Vermin and Rembrandt and Cochise (not Cowboy) flees the station with Swan, Ajax and Snowball. Interestingly, the location for this scene is established as "Broadway and 96th Street" on page 63, yet on the next page the Baseball Furies chase Swan and the others "down 72nd Street" and on page 65 they are suddenly back on 96th Street (the sequence was filmed at the 72nd Street station, which was dressed with 96th Street signage).

In Riverside Park, Cochise is momentarily separated from the others and grabbed by two Furies, who beat him to death and dump his body in the Hudson River. Swan, Ajax and Snowball are pursued through the park by the Furies; because Cowboy does not appear in this sequence as written, it is Ajax alone who becomes winded and must fight the Furies until Swan and Snowball, who veered from the main path, catch up to lend a hand. Swan gets hold of a bat and drops the biggest Fury with a blow to the midsection. The three Warriors easily defeat the other Furies, who retreat and leave the largest Fury behind.

SWAN

Get him up.

Snowball and Ajax pull him to his feet.

SWAN

Get away from him.

Swan holding his bat like a sword.

SWAN

Where's Cochise.

AJAX

They killed him.

Swan raises the bat.

SWAN

I'm not going to ask again.

A long moment.
The Fury shakes his head ...
Then Swan puts out his light.
A sudden, swift movement ...
Next tosses the bat away.
Looks at Snowball and Ajax.

SWAN

Let's go.

There was a change in the Furies' roster early on during the filming of this sequence as well. Stuntman Steve Chambers suffered a broken kneecap and was put on the DL, requiring another fall guy to don pinstripes and Kiss makeup as the "Purple Fury." Aware of Rob Ryder's basketball skills, Hill summoned the athletic location scout to Riverside Park and offered him the job of replacing Chambers, which Ryder accepted, despite having no prior stunt training or experience. The foot chase was still being filmed on the night Ryder first arrived in costume and cleats, but once the fighting started, stunt coordinator Craig Baxley had to quickly bring him up to speed. "He pulled me aside and showed me some stuff," says Ryder. "We choreographed the bat fight with Michael [Beck] and did that, which is when I realized that every time I got hit at the end of a take, I would get a stunt adjustment. I think it was an extra fifty bucks or so. Walter would ask, 'Do you want to do it again?' and I'd say, 'Yeah! Let's do it again!' It was a lot of money at that time, plus I was making something like three hundred and something [dollars] a day through SAG."

The scene between the Fox and Mercy as they walk through the subway tunnel to the next station is almost identical to the same scene between Swan and Mercy in the film, but with two intriguing differences. The first occurs right after Mercy asks to know the Fox's real name, because she likes telling her friends when she's been with somebody "particular"...

THE FOX

Why the hell don't you just tie a mattress to your back ... You don't care where it is, do you ...

MERCY

Well, you're a Warrior. They're big news, they're somebody ...

THE FOX

Yeah, right ...

MERCY

Sure, I know what you guys done at that meeting.

THE FOX

You mean besides running our ass off ...

```
                    MERCY
        You don't have to hide it.
        Anybody who wasted Cyrus ain't
        just anybody.

The Fox stops.

                   THE FOX
        Did what.

                    MERCY
        That's the word going around.
        You guys ... the Warriors ...
        you wasted Cyrus. What's wrong.

He's angry, that's what's wrong.
Very angry.

                   THE FOX
        We got the fuzz chasing our
        ass, now on top of that, every
        gang from here to Coney must
        be looking to come down on us ...
        Some jive bullshit artist gets
        snuffed, we get creamed
        everytime we stick our heads
        out ... and I got one more
        problem. I'm stuck with you.
```

The second difference, more subtextual, comes when Mercy tries to initiate a sexual encounter with the Fox. At first he "gets into it," kissing her and pushing her against the tunnel wall, but when he suddenly pulls away from her she asks him twice, "What's wrong?" before demanding to know, "What is it ... what's wrong with you?" There is a homosexual undercurrent to his reticence that is completely absent from Swan's rebuffing of her in the movie, even though their explanation is basically the same. After all, it is the Fox and not Swan who is consistently the target of Ajax's homophobic slurs, and also the Fox who is closest to Rembrandt, a character played in the film by an effeminate and homosexual actor (Marcelino Sanchez).

Vermin, Cowboy and Rembrandt are the first Warriors to arrive at Union Square. "We just got to sit and wait it out," says Rembrandt. "They'll show up. I know Fox'll show up. He'll figure a way." Vermin and Cowboy notice three "gang chicks" standing across the subway platform, smiling and checking them out (in the movie there are six girls).

Swan, Ajax and Snowball are making their way through Riverside Park when they encounter a nurse sitting alone on a bench listening to a transistor radio. At first, this sequence appears to be taken directly from the novel, except that here the nurse is an undercover policewoman on stakeout and in the book she is a real nurse who drunkenly invites the three Coney Island Dominators to have sex with her in the bushes (and only hollers for the police when Bimbo tries to steal money from her purse).

In the movie, Cochise replaces Cowboy (as originally scripted) in joining Vermin and Rembrandt at the Union Square subway station.

The rest of the scene unfolds identically to the one in the film, except that Snowball is alone when he goes to retrieve Ajax and sees him being arrested.

Heading back to the subway, Swan turns a corner and comes face to face with three members of the Dingos, each with a leashed Doberman. He turns to go back the way he came and is confronted by five more Dingos and five more Dobermans. Described as "bodybuilder types" with "greased up arms" and "skin T-shirts," the Dingos address Swan as "dear" and "honey" and comment on how cute he is. One of the Dingos kicks him twice and tries for a third time, but Swan grabs his leg and breaks it. The other Dingos subdue Swan and take him back to their clubhouse in a straitjacket, where Boss Dingo asks if he has revealed the name of the Warrior who shot Cyrus. The Dingos continue to refer to Swan in the feminine form and again comment on his cuteness, this time while pulling his hair. They show him a gun and tell him they are going to turn him over to the Riffs. He is locked in a room that has a toilet, a small Army cot, two food bowls on the floor (water in one, scraps of food in the other) and a single naked 200-watt light bulb in the ceiling. A small, sealed window of opaque glass is high up in one of the walls and a large open-aperture lock is on the door, close to the knob.

Vermin, Cowboy and Rembrandt leave the Union Square station concourse with the three gang chicks and walk to their clubhouse, which is in a storefront several blocks away. This sequence is slightly different from the one in the film. Rather than being a mostly butch and all-female gang called the Lizzies, the "chicks" here are simply the girlfriends of another gang whose members have yet to return from Cyrus' meeting in the Bronx. As a result, there is nothing homoerotic about this scene as it is presented in the script, though one could argue that Rembrandt's avoidance of these hetero girls says more about his sexuality than the same mistrust he has in the film for the blatantly lesbian Lizzies.

The scripted gang chicks are more effective than their big-screen counterparts. They attack without announcing their motive (the line "So you're the famous Warriors, the guys who shot Cyrus" does not appear in the script), shooting Vermin in the back and killing him and keeping Cowboy and

The Lizzies' aim was truer in the initial script before the originally shot-dead Vermin was allowed to live in the movie.

Rembrandt ignorant of the fact that every gang in the city is looking to waste them.

Back in the Dingos' kennel, Swan smashes the cot, collects one of the screws in his teeth and deposits it in the lock on the door, sharp end pointed up. He rubs the straps of the straitjacket against the screw until they rip, freeing his arms, then climbs out the window. Three stories below: a courtyard and seven sleeping Dobermans. Swan walks along a ledge and shimmies down a drainpipe, which groans loudly from his weight and wakes the Dobermans. Alerted by the barking dogs, Boss Dingo opens a window, spots Swan heading for a tall fence at the end of the ledge and shouts for a gang member named Curt to take action. Curt has a gun and fires four shots at Swan, who makes it over the fence and drops into a trash dumpster at the base of a wall. The Dingos rush the alleyway to recapture him, but he has escaped.

Snowball reunites with Rembrandt and Cowboy at Union Square, and the three go off to look for any other Warriors who may be wandering the station. Meanwhile, the Fox is being tailed by two Big Time Punks—one of them on roller skates—and has led them into the station arcade. When Mercy arrives, she finds six Big Time Punks with their eyes on the Fox, who is playing a 10-cent Mr. Top Gun mechanical quick-draw shooting game (in the novel, Hinton plays a similar game in the Times Square subway arcade). The rest room fight is the same, except there are four Warriors instead of six (Vermin and Cochise are dead) going against six Big Time Punks rather than nine in the film.

The subway ride back to Coney Island features more dialogue among the four Warriors and Mercy, most of it centered around the Fox's growing disillusionment with gang life and his encouragement of Rembrandt's artistic expression ("Don't let go of your spray can," he tells the youngest Warrior. "It's your passport in case you want to get out"). The short encounter with the two couples is the same, with one of the women dropping her corsage. When the Warriors reach the Stillwell Avenue station and disembark, the Fox gives Mercy the corsage. She asks again for his real name, and this time he acquiesces: His name is Francis Conroy.

After the Cadillac hearse pulls up and follows the Warriors toward the boardwalk, the Fox identifies the occupants as the Rogues and—just like in the cemetery scene—tells the others that they are the gang responsible for killing Cyrus. (In the film, he never IDs the Rogues at all, leaving a question mark at the end as to how Swan knows they are the real killers and not just another gang looking to waste the Warriors.) Cowboy and Rembrandt want to run away, and the Fox wonders where they're planning to run to. For a moment, the Warriors are without leadership and lost on their own turf.

```
A long pause.
They look at one another.

                    SNOWBALL
          Let's get even.

It's the first time he's ever spoken.
```

COWBOY

Hey, nobody ever thought you had a tongue.

SNOWBALL

Let's get even for Cyrus... For Cleon, for Vermin, for Cochise, for Ajax... for Swan.

Tension building.

THE FOX

Why not.

REMBRANDT

We got to.

COWBOY

Yeah... Fuck the fucking Rogues. I'm ready to bop.

Swan reappears while the four Warriors are gathering weapons in preparation for a rumble with the Rogues. He leads the gang to the beach

Luther learns that you can win by bringing a knife to a gunfight.

for the final confrontation, where his speed and accuracy with a knife pays off against gun-toting Luther, in homage to the climactic showdown in Akira Kurosawa's *Yojimbo* (1961), where Toshiro Mifune's antihero similarly disarms baddie Tatsuya Nakadai (Hill would go on to remake the influential action classic a decade and a half later as *Last Man Standing*). The screenplay ends like the film, except that the Fox and Mercy are together on the beach and Swan is standing alone, staring out at the sea.

4 Criticism and Controversy: *The Warriors* Hits the Streets

Cinematic history is full of movies that were put down by the critics of their day, only to become either immediately popular successes or gradually building cult favorites. All three, as it turns out, were true of *The Warriors*, which was disdained by the majority of reviewers at the time, was a box-office hit right out of the gate and then built an enthusiastic, devoted and enduring following after that.

Interestingly, given what was to immediately follow the film's release, *The Warriors* did not receive much in the way of initial criticism for its violent content, or its potential to inspire the same in its viewers. Nonetheless, Paramount hedged their bets regarding the reaction and didn't offer journalists the opportunity to see the film in advance. *Variety*'s "Poll" reported, "There was no pre-release trade-screening of *The Warriors*, ostensibly due to last-minute editing and an unavailability of prints. That explanation doesn't hold up, however, since Paramount opened the film in 670 venues...and it takes at least two weeks for that many prints to be struck. More likely explanation is fear of a repeat of the critical drubbing Hill and producer Lawrence Gordon took on their previous pic, *The Driver*."

Also noting the studio's lack of faith was one of the only major reviewers to throw unequivocal support behind *The Warriors*: the celebrated Pauline Kael in *The New Yorker*. In her last review for the magazine before departing to accept a stint as a consultant to Paramount, at the invitation of no less than Warren Beatty—though she would be back at *The New*

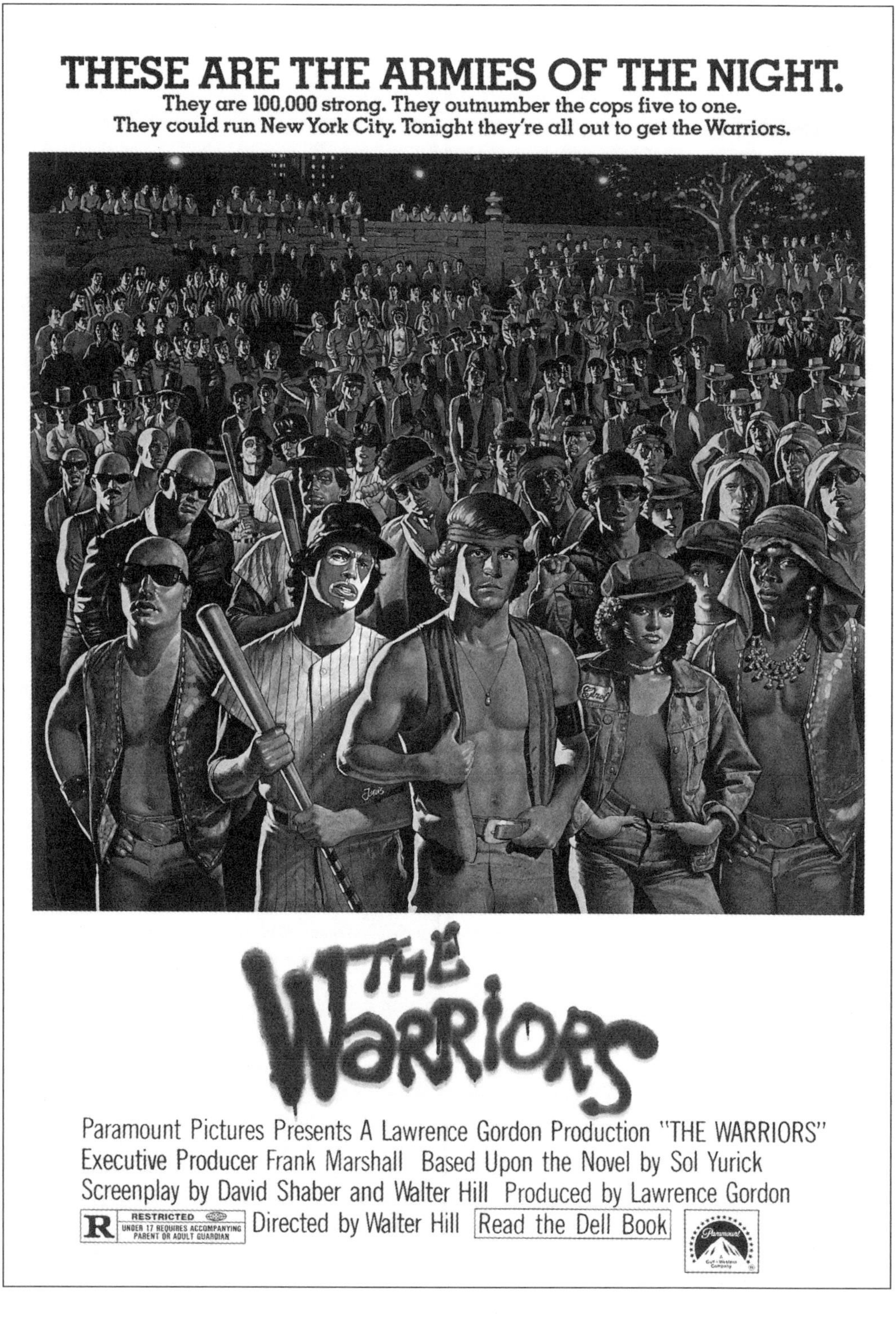

THESE ARE THE ARMIES OF THE NIGHT.

They are 100,000 strong. They outnumber the cops five to one.
They could run New York City. Tonight they're all out to get the Warriors.

Paramount Pictures Presents A Lawrence Gordon Production "THE WARRIORS"
Executive Producer Frank Marshall Based Upon the Novel by Sol Yurick
Screenplay by David Shaber and Walter Hill Produced by Lawrence Gordon
R RESTRICTED UNDER 17 REQUIRES ACCOMPANYING PARENT OR ADULT GUARDIAN Directed by Walter Hill Read the Dell Book

Yorker within a year—Kael, a supporter of Hill's previous work, wrote, "Probably the assumption was that the audience for this picture doesn't read reviews. But the literate shouldn't miss out on it. *The Warriors* is a real moviemaker's movie."

Among the few who did attack the film on the grounds of potential incitefulness was the *Pittsburgh Press*' Ed Blank: "*The Warriors* is the supreme glorification of antisocial behavior...The picture is attracting an audience that revels in its viciousness. The making and exhibition of *The Warriors* is an act of irresponsibility." Not surprisingly, the U.S. Catholic Conference, reviewing *The Warriors* in its *Film & Broadcasting Review*, concurred, slapping it with a C (Condemned) rating and saying, "The picture's constant violence and, more significantly, its glorification of vicious behavior are seriously offensive."

The gang cliches are all here in a weak 'Warriors'

'Warriors' Gangs Up On Unwary Audience

Another who objected to the mayhem, albeit on the grounds of romanticizing it as opposed to explicitness of presentation, was *The Chicago Tribune*'s Gene Siskel, who rated it one star. After putting down the "X-rated cartoon style" of the dialogue, he wrote, "You would think after watching *The Warriors* that gang membership was a victimless crime... This entire film is a romantic lie." Across town at the *Chicago Sun-Times*, Roger Ebert gave it a slightly more generous two stars, decrying the stylization of its urban characters and locales: "There's hardly a moment when we believe that the movie's gangs are real or that their members are real people or that they inhabit a real city...[A]ction audiences, I suspect, will find it either incomprehensible or laughable."

In fact, a number of critics took Hill to task for emphasizing action, movement and imagery rather than mounting a serious look at the problem of gang warfare. "By deciding to only capture the 'flavor' of gang life, the film's creator unconsciously declares himself incapable of dealing with the real issues at hand," wrote the *Philadelphia Daily News*' Joe Baltake. "*The Warriors* doesn't even try to make a statement; it simply records trash-can ambience and nonstop energy." Among the few with positive things to say about Hill's *mise-en-scène* was Janet Maslin in *The New York Times*: "Mr. Hill uses subways, jukeboxes, spectacularly eerie costumes and deserted streets to create a stark yet extravagant visual style, and a grimy little world in which everything looks curiously brand-new."

Then there were the critics who covered it after the real-life trouble started (more on that shortly), and couldn't resist using it as a platform from which to take potshots at the movie. "Considering that *The Warriors* is a bit of phantasmagoric nonsense," wrote Dick Shippy in the *Akron Beacon-Journal*, "...perhaps the punks were reacting to having been ripped off for four bucks to watch a perfectly good rumble degenerate into an allegorical mess?" In Michigan's *Times Herald*, Mary Harris chimed in with, "*The Warriors* is dull, clichéd, and by no stretch of the imagination sensational... The only possible explanation for the bizarre behavior this film has engendered is that its audiences felt bored and ripped off."

The fuss about 'Warriors' evades her; it's just boring

On the other hand, when *The Village Voice*'s Andrew Sarris caught the film two weeks after it opened, in the wake of all the headlines, he observed, "Media outrage once more seems to be much ado about very little. The panic of the studios is depressingly familiar. My instinctive tendency to oppose all censorship...has not even been seriously tested." In Kael's review, her take on the controversy was more pointed: "If there's an immutable law about movies, it may be that middle-class people get hot and bothered whenever there's a movie that the underclass really responds to."

And respond they did. After it opened on February 9, 1979, *The Warriors* was number one at the box-office in its first weekend, grossing $3.5 million (a very respectable figure back in those days of much smaller wide releases) and knocking Richard Donner's *Superman* (1978) from its perch at the top of the charts. But no sooner had that opening frame concluded than that success would be tarnished by real-life events that would mar its immediate reputation, and yet assure its notoriety and longevity.

On the evening of February 12, 1979, 19-year-old Marvin Kenneth Eller went to see *The Warriors* with some friends at the Palm Springs Drive-In in California. They got into an altercation with another group of youths, shots were fired, and Eller was struck in the head. He was taken to hospital, and died four days later.

That same night, 18-year-old Thomas Gitchell also joined a few pals at a showing of *The Warriors* at the Esplanade Theater in Oxnard, CA. There, a similar confrontation resulted in Gitchell and two other young men being stabbed, Gitchell fatally. And then, three nights later (as detailed in this book's introduction), Martin Yakubowicz lost his life in Massachusetts.

The press jumped all over these stories, and *The Warriors* quickly became the poster child for the pernicious influence of violent cinema. Hooliganism in theaters showing films about teenage bad behavior was nothing new; most famously, showings of Richard Brooks' juvenile-delinquent classic *Blackboard Jungle* (1955), with its trailblazing rock 'n' roll soundtrack, were followed by incidents of vandalism. This was different, though: *The Warriors* had a body count, and the papers and TV news broadcasts had a field day, some mourning the loss of good, hardworking young men, others offering lurid, second-hand details (it was suggested in some quarters that Eller and others involved in his incident were members of the infamous motorcycle club the Hells Angels). These accounts were followed, inevitably, by thinkpieces mulling over the causal relationship between cinema and societal violence, who was responsible for it, and what should be done about it.

No more deaths followed, but the unfortunate incidents continued. One that didn't get as much press, most likely because a fatality wasn't involved, saw Richard Alley, the manager of the State Theater in Pasadena, CA, fall victim to assault by one of several groups of youths who had been fighting in the lobby on February 14 while *The Warriors* was playing. The rest of the evening's shows were cancelled, though Lori Ham, the assistant manager who took over for Alley, didn't jump to the conclusion that the movie was responsible. "That night we just happened to get a bunch of people in here who hated each other," she told the *Los Angeles Times*' Charles Schreger. "As far as I'm concerned, they were just a group of stupid idiots who came in loaded. The same thing could have happened if they were in a bowling alley together." At another Oxnard theater, the Sky View Drive-In, a night's showings had to be cancelled due to fog, some patrons revolted, and the police were called in.

Movie Glorifies Gang Violence, Group Charges

EXTRA SECURITY

Keeping an Eye on 'Warriors'

The Warriors also attracted the attention of an unsanctioned law-and-order group that would soon become a *cause célèbre* in Manhattan. A theater showing the movie in Times Square was picketed by the Magnificent 13, an anti-crime initiative (which would be rechristened with its better-known moniker The Guardian Angels later that year) headed by then-23-year-old Curtis Sliwa. He had no love for the film, describing it to the Associated Press as "violence from front to end, lacking a plot. It preaches organized gang violence and leaves you with the thought that organized gangs can rule this city. The bad guys are cops and the good guys are gangs. Where is everyone else?"

A few days after *The Warriors* opened, three of the film's stars—Michael Beck, David Harris, and Terry Michos—went together to watch it with an audience on 42nd Street (the film was playing at the New Amsterdam Theatre with another controversial Paramount release, Michael Winner's *Death Wish* [1974], as its second feature). "Once it opened, a couple of us went and sat in the back with an audience on 42nd Street who were talking to the screen," Beck told *Shock Cinema*'s Paul Talbot. "And it was very cool because none of us had a track record in movies and you're in this movie and you're seeing people viscerally react. It was very exciting to see the audience respond."

"They were going nuts," Michos agrees. "People were yelling at the screen, saying, 'I don't know how to fight, but man, these guys...' They were gang members!" After the movie ended and the three stars were walking out, Michos remembers one of those gang members recognizing Beck in the lobby. "He said, 'Hey, you look like that guy!' Michael said, 'Y'know, people tell me that all the time. That's why I came to see the film—I wanted to see who this guy was.' Then he said [to us], 'Let's get out of here.' " The trio beat a hasty retreat before anyone else spotted them.

Across the five boroughs, meanwhile, journalists ventured to various theaters to find out first-hand if and how *The Warriors* was shaping behavior in the city where it was filmed. The *New York Post*'s Sam Rosensohn spoke to the (unidentified) manager of the Elmwood theater in Queens, who said of the movie's audience, "They come in with leather jackets, some have chains, knives and who knows what else. So far nobody's got stabbed or shot in the head, but it's come pretty close." At the RKO Fordham One in Bronx, assistant manager Adrian Pagan said, "We came close to having a fight between the staff and five other guys, all because of the movie. They get too rowdy... Some guys pulled out a switchblade, and one of the ushers got threatened with a knife." In the same article, one of those ushers, Miguel Hernandez, claimed that the only thing preventing gang warfare in his theater was that its patrons were aware that the ushers knew martial arts. Similarly, a *Daily News* story by Jack Leahy and Arthur Mulligan, after offering accounts of two attacks on the staff of Queens' RKO Keith's theater, revealed that the manager of the Elmwood had a black belt in judo!

Over at the RKO Kenmore in Brooklyn, the head security guard of a detail hired to keep the place safe during *The Warriors*' run told *The Village Voice*'s Arthur Bell that the movie was definitely luring, if not starting, trouble.

"There have been fights this week, but we move them outside. Probably every youth gang in Brooklyn has been here for this one. They go in noisy, they try to take over the theatre. The movie makes them do bad things."

One scribe went even further, talking to actual NYC street gangs to get their takes on the film. In the *Daily News*, NYPD cop turned Police Athletic League counselor Joe Gallick interviewed members of Brooklyn outfits the Sex Boys and the Crazy Homicides, and one of the latter suggested a measure of restraint in his crew's reaction: "There was another gang in the theater when we saw *The Warriors*. They were wearing their colors, but there was no confrontation. If we were jitterbugging, you'd see a lot of people flying off the balcony." Brother Louie of Sex Boys was more philosophical: "[The movie] showed people that there are other ways of living. It shows them another part of life in the ghetto. You know, being a warrior, or an outlaw or whatever."

Up in Boston, there were much stronger repercussions following the Yakubowicz murder. The film came under fire from State Sen. Michael LoPresti, who spearheaded an effort to get *The Warriors* banned in Boston. "I thought the film artistically was awful," he raged to the *L.A. Times*' Schreger, "and while I've seen gorier films, I think it glorifies violence too

Two street gangs give their blessings to a wild new film

WARRIORS

By JOE GALLICK

OVER THE YEARS, the Sex Boys and the Crazy Homicides have had their disagreements. Two years ago, the Brooklyn-based Hispanic gangs met at the corner of Milford and Glenmore Aves. in East New York. An estimated 45 rounds of gunfire were exchanged during a 30-minute war that rained bullets from the windows and rooftops of the surrounding tenements. Three gang members and five 13th Division of the Crazy Homicides in East New York. By now, on a citywide level, the gang has an estimated 500 members, all armed with automatic weapons.

"The posters about 'The Warriors' got my attention," said Diamond. "I wanted to see their colors (uniforms)."

He also heard the ads saying that the gang was from Brooklyn. "I wanted to see if anyone in the movie looked familiar."

In "The Warriors," a young black messiah named Cyrus calls for a peaceful assembly of all street gangs. They meet in the North Bronx. He appeals to them to unite and take over the city, pointing out that they are 60,000 strong and there are only 20,000 cops. "Can you count suckers?" he urges them on. "The future is ours — can you dig it?!"

Cyrus is gunned down by a member of "The Rogues" at the most dramatic part of his speech but it is "The Warriors" who are blamed. The movie focuses on the gang's attempt to return to Brooklyn via the much." He contacted the Massachusetts Attorney General and the Suffolk County district attorney, hoping to get the movie banned in the Boston area or perhaps rerated to an X, though Motion Picture Association of America president Jack Valenti told Schreger there wasn't much chance of that: "The ratings board can only rate what is on the screen, not what's in people's minds."

The Fields Corner Station in Dorchester, Boston (site of the Martin Yakubowicz stabbing) today.

At a special hearing set up by LoPresti at Boston's state house to address the *Warriors* problem, National Association of Theater Owners president A. Alan Friedberg, speaking on behalf of Saxon owner Sack Theatres, defended the freedom of exhibitors to show whatever movies they chose. "There is not a casual relationship between films and real life," he said in *Variety*. "Motion pictures are a mirror, a reflection of the real world in which we live. To change that is to change the behavior of citizens. The world is what it is. It's the films that reflect the real world. To pin it [violence] on a film or television is begging the question. We are talking about sick, demented people who would have done what they did anyway."

No conclusion was reached at the hearing, and *The Warriors* continued to play at the Saxon to solid business. In other Massachusetts cities, though, local officials succeeded in getting *The Warriors* ejected from area theaters, including the Billerica Mall Cinemas and Route 3 Cinemas in Chelmsford. Chelmsford police chief James Greska told *Variety*, "There was rowdyism and a lot of shouting by groups of young people coming out of the theater... People are concerned when they read about the killing and beatings after the movie showed in other towns. Shutting down the movie would have been a violation of the First Amendment, but I don't think the film does anybody any good."

In 1981, Yakubowicz's father William filed a lawsuit against Paramount and the Sack Theatres chain (identified as the Saxon Theater Corporation), represented by attorneys Don Lubin and Elizabeth Mulvey, who charged that both *The Warriors* and its advertising were "directed to producing imminent lawless acts of violence." Part of the claim stated that Barrett had quoted the film's dialogue by yelling, "I want you, I'm going to get you!" as he challenged Yakubowicz, though Paramount's attorneys countered that this threat is not, in fact, spoken by anyone in the film. (This did not stop several news outlets from reporting Barrett's "imitation" as fact.)

The suit also charged that Paramount and Sack Theatres were negligent in not warning potential patrons of the dangers involved in attending *The Warriors*, given the violence in California a few days prior. According to *Variety*, part of the argument was that the studio and exhibitor bore the same form of responsibility in Yakubowicz's slaying as that of a bartender who served a drunk driver before a fatal accident. (It is thus a tad ironic that, according to the trade, the studio's defense included the report of an eyewitness who claimed that Barrett was so intoxicated during the movie that he passed out and didn't even see most of it!)

In April 1989—a full 10 years after the murder—the Massachusetts Supreme Court determined that "The plaintiff in a civil action did not demonstrate that the defendants, a motion picture producer and the operator of a movie theatre, violated their duty of reasonable care to members of the public with respect to the creation and exhibition of a certain film, *The Warriors*," and that "A fatal assault committed by a theatre patron several miles from the theatre at which, a short time earlier, he had viewed a certain film, could not, as matter of law, be attributed to an alleged failure by the producer of the film to 'protect [people] at or near the theatre' or to warn the theatre operator or public officials of the dangers of film-related violence." The decision further stated, "Although the film is rife with violent scenes, it does not at any point exhort, urge, entreat, solicit or overtly advocate or encourage unlawful or violent activity on the part of viewers. It does not create the likelihood or inciting or producing 'imminent lawless action' that would strip the film of First Amendment protection."

The court was far from the first to express this opinion; some journalists and observers picked up that flag not long after *The Warriors*' release and the ensuing troubles. Unsurprisingly, industry exhibitor publication *Boxoffice* led the charge when it came to articles downplaying the influence of *The Warriors* on its more violent patrons. The trade sampled theater owners and managers in Dayton, OH, Easton, PA, and Stamford, CT, and reported that no serious incidents had occurred at any of those locales. Another story, by Ron Schaumburg, emphasized that the California killings were not directly sparked by the movie. The Palm Springs incident, according to a police sergeant, had nothing to do with gang rivalry (involving the Hells Angels or anyone else) and instead stemmed from black youths stopping a white girl from entering a rest room. Similarly, interracial tensions had led to the fight that claimed Gitchell's life. One *Boxoffice* item even revealed that at Phoenix, AZ's Tower Plaza Mall Cinema, manager Morton Berger and his staff costumed themselves after some of the film's most outrageously dressed characters, and had no problems despite drawing sellout crowds at every weekend evening show.

A New York story that arose about *The Warriors* proved to be exaggerated as well. A dozen of the movie's young patrons were reported to have descended into the subway station at 42nd Street and 8th Avenue and terrorized innocent people on the platform, but a *New York Times* piece later quoted the transit patrolmen who had arrested them as saying that they were picked up for turnstile jumping only, and hadn't bothered any passengers.

Dirty dozen see 'Warriors' & ape film in IND

Nevertheless, in response to all the negative publicity, Paramount vice president in charge of distribution Frank Mancuso (whose son Frank Jr. would soon spearhead the *Friday the 13th* sequels) told *Variety*, "Paramount does not want to exploit in any way a regrettable situation that has developed." The studio cancelled *The Warriors*' nationwide advertising campaign on February 16, pulling the movie's TV and radio spots—though not, as *Variety* pointed out in another story, the large subway ads that would be most visible to actual gang members. (The studio also let exhibitors know that they were free to cancel the film if they felt their venues were at risk for violence, and offered to pick up the tab for any additional security that theaters might want to employ—asking their owners to wait until the end of the movie's run before billing them.)

Gone also was the menacing newspaper ad art, echoing that seen on the posters, depicting an endless mass of fierce-looking gang members and emblazoned with the tagline "These are the armies of the night." Instead, new print ads that debuted the following Thursday the 22nd simply ran the title logo with "*The Warriors* can be seen at these theaters, at these times," plus a theater directory—and a larger R-rating logo.

Other new marketing emphasized the positive critical response. Kael's rave from *The New Yorker* ran in its entirety in ads appearing in *The New*

THE WARRIORS — They rumbled into town . . . were kicked out . . . but they're back again

York Times, the *Los Angeles Times* and elsewhere the first Friday in March. Another tactic employed by the studio was to reprint sections of a Maslin follow-up piece from *The New York Times* downplaying any objectionable content: "Its ads make it look almost too scary: for every blood-and-guts buff who's been drawn in by scenes of teenage gangs swarming through the subways swinging baseball bats, a less adventuresome soul has surely been scared away. In fact, these ads are hopelessly misleading, since 'The Warriors' is a meticulous, terrific-looking movie a lot less rowdy than the average Western."

Meanwhile, her fellow *Times* reviewer Vincent Canby weighed in on *The Warriors* in the wake of the crimes, the resulting in-print hand-wringing over the relationship between reel and real mayhem, and Paramount's responsibility in the unfortunate events. In a piece titled "When a Tame Film Inspires Violence" in the March 4, 1979 edition, he asked, "...why should it—rather than any number of other films far more furious, vicious and violent, such as *Death Wish*—be associated with the sort of lethal events that took place two weeks ago in California and Massachusetts? … There is absolutely nothing I can see in *The Warriors*—after the fact—that explains the phenomenon. … *The Warriors* is such a mish-mash of romantic clichés, moods and visual effects that it's difficult to understand how it could inflame anyone not a close relative of a cast or crew member. … In both [major fight scenes] there is much use of clubs, knives, fists and karate chops, yet no one is permanently or even seriously injured. … How could this movie incite anything except skepticism? I'm baffled."

He wasn't alone in the critical field in taking this point of view. Around the same time, Ebert, who frequently stood apart from general consensuses blaming movies for antisocial behavior, opined in the *Sun-Times* that the heightened nature of *The Warriors*' presentation of gang life made it unlikely to have sparked imitative behavior in its viewers. "The audiences seem to like the movie not in spite of its lack of realism, but because of it. … The stylized, rough elegance of *The Warriors* provides an alternative fantasy world… Given the nature of the street gang members, isn't it possible that the fights started because the gangs were in the same place at the same time, and hostility followed from that? … It's more likely that gangs are going to see 'themselves' on the screen and then behaving, afterwards, as they probably would have anyway."

For his part, actor Michael Garfield Levine was surprised by the hullabaloo that greeted his feature-film debut. "To me, it was just a movie about New York City," he says. "That's how I looked at it, 'cause I was born and raised there, and it was the '70s and I was just starting out my career, and I honestly didn't think a heck of a lot about the content too much. I mean, there have always been gangs in New York, and tons of ethnic and racial and socioeconomic disparities."

"You know, I don't like violence," his co-star Thomas G. Waites offers. "I don't think it solves anything. And certainly, anything that glorifies violence is probably not a good idea. But then you limit the scope of an artist's expression. I think *The Warriors* just hit that edge where it was Walter's vision to make it theatrical, and Craig Baxley's fight choreography was way ahead of his time. The blend of that and Walter's vision was beautiful, but they hit society at a time when violence was lurking beneath the surface. Which is what art is supposed to do: It's supposed to express what's going on in society. I do think that the popularity of gang life increased after that. I mean, who had ever heard of the Crips and the Bloods, you know, and all of a sudden they became household names."

Actor Joel Weiss reveals that the uproar over *The Warriors* cost him a rather unlikely follow-up gig. "After the movie was a box-office hit for three weeks, my manager got me [the game show] *Hollywood Squares*—with David Patrick Kelly sharing the square! Then I was watching Rona Barrett, who used to do the gossip thing on ABC [*Good Morning America*], at like 8:30 in the morning, and she began by talking about how people were dying because of *The Warriors*, and they were pulling the [advertising]. So I never did *Hollywood Squares*. And David and I weren't even Warriors, we were Rogues!"

Just as things were starting to simmer down in the United States, more controversy was stirred up over in France. A public march against unemployment in downtown Paris had led to hooliganism among high-school-aged participants, a number of whom were arrested and jailed, so sensitivity to youth street violence was at a high. In the midst of this strife, the country's Minister of Culture and Communications, Philippe Lecat, followed the advice of his control commission and branded *The Warriors*, which had been set for release that summer, with an X rating. At the time, the X was a separate classification from an "adults only" tag; movies given the former could only play on the hardcore adult-theater circuit, and were subject to additional taxes and duties. Around that time, Larry Cohen's *God Told Me To* (1976) was also given an X—as much for its "blasphemous" content as for its bloodshed—which Lecat switched to "adults only" after an appeal from the local distributor.

Daniel Goldman, the Paris head of Cinema International Corp., *The Warriors*' French distributor, wasn't as fortunate. "We are protesting to the minister and asking that the commission should be told to reconsider their classification," he told *Variety*; part of his argument involved citing other international openings that were unaccompanied by any violent outbursts. But the X held, and Goldman wound up cutting 10 minutes from the movie in order for it to play mainstream theaters. It finally opened August 27, 1980 and did solid business, with no incidents reported—which is not to say Goldman's decision wasn't attacked. Local critics who had seen the uncut *Warriors* at the Deauville Film Festival the previous year chided him, and Hill himself wrote an open letter to the country's filmgoers that appeared in the newsweekly *L'Express*:

"The cuts made by the censor on The Warriors *force me to reject all authorship of the version currently being shown in Paris. I don't wish to make a special plea for my motion picture. I simply wish to add my name to the long list that believes what can happen to one film can happen to all films, that believes when one freedom is abridged all freedoms are endangered; that believes censorship is an insult to the dignity of the individual and an insult to the idea of democracy."*

Goldman responded by telling *Variety*, "If I spent over a year fighting for the film, it's because I love it and think it would be a shame if it were not seen here. I don't believe the light cuts we made harm the film."

Beyond all the uproar, *The Warriors* attracted journalistic attention—and a bit of apprehension—for another reason: It was the first of a string of studio productions dealing with gang life and youth crime scheduled for release the same year. (Though it was not specifically a gang movie, the huge success of John Badham's *Saturday Night Fever* [1977] was cited as a key factor in jumpstarting the trend.) These ranged from Philip Kaufman's *The Wanderers*, a somewhat more benign nostalgia piece set in the 1963 Bronx and based on Richard Price's novel, to Tim Hunter's *Over the Edge*, a cautionary drama about restless, bored, underserved youth in a planned community eventually erupting into rebellion. The film, which marked Matt Dillon's screen debut, was a victim of lingering concerns about imitative behavior engendered by *The Warriors*, and never got a proper theatrical release, though it has since become a cult favorite.

Another pair of movies zeroed in on the barrios of Los Angeles, and softened the material with romantic elements. Robert Collins' *Walk Proud*, originally and much more bluntly titled *Gang!* and scripted by *The Blackboard Jungle*'s Evan Hunter, stars a very incongruously cast Robby Benson as a Hispanic East L.A. gang member who falls for a Caucasian girl and tries to escape the life. Michael Pressman's *Boulevard Nights* more appropriately features Richard Yniguez and Danny De La Paz as brothers Raymond and Chuco, whose relationship is threatened by the latter's gang involvement. Part of the film's focus is on Raymond's engagement to his girlfriend Shady (Marta DuBois), and Warner Bros. VP Joe Hyams told entertainment columnist Marilyn Beck, "I suppose the love element of the story can't take the heat off of it. I'm not saying it's as inflammatory as *The Warriors*, but I would assume there will now be some re-evaluation of the picture in light of the events occurring with the Paramount film."

Indeed, when Ebert reviewed *Boulevard Nights*, he reported encountering a protest group claiming movies like this and *The Warriors* were "part of a plot by the 'fascist ruling class' to 'poison the minds of thousands.' " And even though, as Ebert noted, *Nights* takes a more thoughtful approach to the gang situation, it too was marked by assaults at its venues, though these incidents didn't attract nearly the attention of those associated with *The Warriors*.

Unforeseen violence haunts teen-gang movie producers

Four youths were shot and another stabbed outside the Alhambra Theater in San Francisco; two girls were stabbed and a boy was shot in Ontario, CA; and 11 youths were arrested after a gang-related fight at a San Jose drive-in. *Boulevard Nights* was pulled from those theaters, and, echoing Paramount's response to the *Warriors* fatalities, Warner Bros. offered to provide free security to other houses showing their film.

Also in '79, Timothy Galfas' supposedly NYC-set *Sunnyside,* starring Joey (older brother of John) Travolta as the leader of a street gang called the Nightcrawlers, sparked anger among residents of the real Sunnyside section of Queens, who felt the movie misrepresented their neighborhood as being rife with gang violence. In response, members of the community's planning board staged protests outside theaters in the borough that were showing the movie, but it was much ado about nothing: Sunnyside is never identified by name in the movie, which was mostly filmed in Los Angeles (the *Variety* review mentions visible palm trees and barely concealed California license plates) and produced by someone who had never even set foot in that part of Queens.

Two more films featured street gangs as villainous supporting characters. In Stephen Verona's *Boardwalk* (1979), Ruth Gordon and Lee Strasberg play longtime Coney Island residents threatened by the arrival of a vicious gang leader. John Flynn's *Defiance* (1980) toplines Jan-Michael Vincent as a merchant seaman who moves into a Lower East Side neighborhood and wages war against the local thugs.

Also noted in the coverage of this trend was *American Me*, a script written by Floyd Mutrux in 1973 that traced 30 years of the Latino gang experience and had become a hot property, selling to Universal and attracting Al Pacino to star. The studio shelved the project, but production executive Sean Daniel pulled it out of limbo in '77 and cast Edward James Olmos in the lead, with Hal Ashby and then Mutrux himself set to direct. The movie wouldn't be produced until over a decade later, however; it was released in 1992, with Olmos both starring and directing. (At least one article also cited *Gangs of New York*, in development by Martin Scorsese and screenwriter Jay Cocks even back then!) Ironically, the '79 picture that could be viewed as *The Warriors*' closest cinematic cousin—George Miller's blistering, kinetically stylized *Mad Max*—was nowhere to be seen in these articles, as it was at the time a low-profile production that had yet to make a splash in its home country of Australia, much less in the States.

Soon after *The Warriors* was pulled from theaters, a few gang-related films that had initially failed to recoup their costs were given second chances in theaters, some with revamped marketing strategies. One such film was *Cat Murkil and the Silks*, a brutal low-budgeter that had premiered in 1976 and fizzled at the box office, likely due to its awkward title and outdated promotional copy ("From confidential police files... THE SHOCKING STORY OF TEENAGE GANGS"). Rebranded as *Cruisin' High* in 1977 by a different distributor, the film found new life during the gang movie boom and remained in regional release as late as 1980. *Youngblood,* a gang movie AIP had released in May 1978, continued to play in sub-run theaters and drive-ins with a tag line that mentioned "gang wars." The fact that it starred Lawrence Hilton-Jacobs (from the popular sitcom *Welcome Back, Kotter*) and featured a soundtrack by the funk band War also helped its marketability in urban venues.

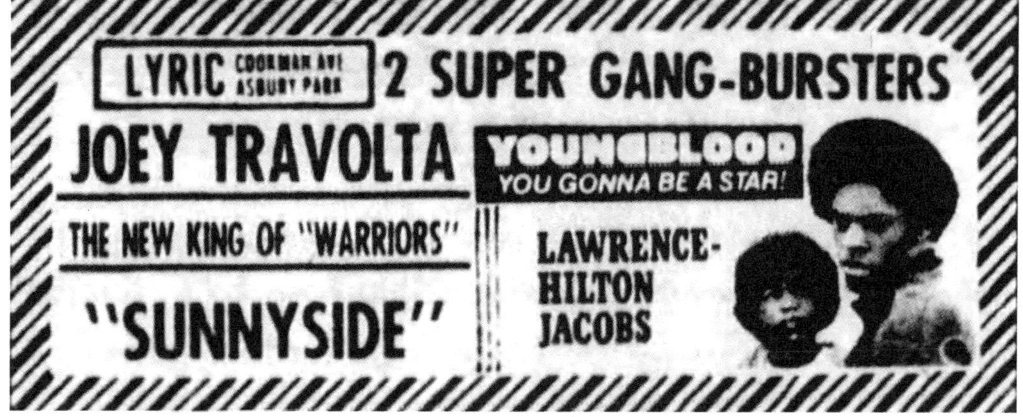

Then there was the string of movies that, in content and/or advertising, sincerely flattered *The Warriors* via imitation. *Devil's Express* (1976) was a martial arts/horror hybrid about a Harlem karate instructor who travels to Hong Kong for training and unknowingly brings home an ancient amulet that unleashes a bug-eyed demon into the New York subway system. A subplot in which several warring gangs are blamed for the demon's killing spree opened the door for distributor Cinematic Releasing to reissue the film as *Gang Wars* in July 1979. The new ad campaign not only aped the *Warriors*' "These are the armies of the night" tagline with the slightly modified "These are the real gangs of the night," but also copied the iconic angled text of the *Star Wars* logo.

The Toei Company of Japan fast-tracked their own cash-in production shortly after the studio's CEO, Shigeru Okada, caught a showing of *The Warriors* during a business trip to the U.S. The result was *Violent Warrior* [*Boryoku senshi*], a scrappy 16mm quickie written and directed by Teruo Ishii, known for his lurid *ero guro* [erotic grotesque] films like *Orgies of Edo*

and *Horrors of Malformed Men* (both 1969). It kicks off with a chaotic brawl at a rock concert in Kobe between the Street Fighters from Tokyo and a local gang, the Doberman Kids. During the melee, Ken, the leader of the Street Fighters, and Maria, the younger sister of the Doberman Kids' leader, are arrested and handcuffed together.

Their subsequent escape launches a wild chase through discos, shopping malls, pachinko parlors, warehouses, shipyards, railyards, beaches, marinas, and—of course—subway stations and trains. As Ken and the Street Fighters bop their way back with Maria in tow, they encounter face-painted gangs patterned after the Baseball Furies and the Lizzies, a roller derby team, and a bunch of guys on 10-speed bicycles who fire pachinko balls at them with slingshots. Toei released *Violent Warrior* on October 6, 1979, three weeks after *The Warriors* premiered in Japan, co-billed with *Angel's Desire* [*Tenshi No Yokubō*], the studio's knockoff of another controversial Paramount release, *Looking for Mr. Goodbar* (1977).

Steven Jacobson's *Team-Mates*, a microbudgeted teen comedy about an athletically inclined girl who joins her high school's football team to get back at her cheating boyfriend, who also happens to be the team captain, was a box-office failure during its initial release in 1978. But a subplot about a gang of toughs called the Cougars who are always getting into

These faux Baseball Furies show up in *Violent Warrior* (1979) for a 10-minute action sequence, but are nowhere to be found in the trailers or publicity photos for this Japanese *Warriors* cash-in.

trouble with the athletes was justification enough for producer Sam Sherman to repackage the movie as *Young Gangs* in 1980. Three years later, after *Fast Times at Ridgemont High* became a surprise hit, Sherman changed the ad campaign again and put it back in theaters as *Young Gangs from Wildwood High*. Whatever its title, the movie is only remembered today for containing the feature debuts of James Spader (who was a teenager at the time) and *Golden Girls* star Estelle Getty.

In 1981, Jack Hill's *Switchblade Sisters* (originally released in 1975 and a.k.a. *The Jezebels*) returned to drive-ins and grindhouses as *Playgirl Gang*, on double and triple bills with other Motion Picture Marketing retitle jobs like *Vampire Playgirls* (a.k.a. *The Devil's Nightmare*), *Eager Beavers* (a.k.a. *The Swinging Barmaids*), and *Graveyard Tramps* (a.k.a. *Invasion of the Bee Girls*). But that vague suggestion of a connection was nothing compared to *Sisters*' release in Spain, both theatrically and on video, as *The Warriors II: Las Navajeras*!

The posters and newspaper ads for William Lustig's *Vigilante* (1983) depicted not righteously armed leads Robert Forster and Fred William-

son, but a small army of the night quite reminiscent of the one in *The Warriors'* marketing. The point was made even finer when Lustig's movie was rechristened *Street Gang* midway through its theatrical run, and when it opened in Germany as *Street Fighters* with a one-sheet suggesting that the pictured gang were the heroes, not the villains.

April 1983 saw the U.S. release of another Williamson-starrer, *1990: The Bronx Warriors*, which had opened in its native Italy the previous October. Enzo G. Castellari, just coming off his notorious *Jaws* imitation *The Last Shark/Great White* (1981), directed this catch-all cash-in on *The Warriors*, *Escape from New York*, and the *Mad Max* movies. It's set in the titular borough that is now a "No Man's Land" inhabited by colorful rival gangs with names like the Riders, the Tigers, the Zombies (who get around on roller-skates like the leader of *The Warriors'* Punks), and the Scavengers. Its hero, Trash (Mark Gregory), has a romance with outsider girl Ann (Stefania Girolami)—but theirs does not end nearly as happily as Swan and Mercy's in *The Warriors*.

The Warriors' influence continued to be felt on the B-movie scene a decade later, in Richard W. Munchkin's *Ring of Fire II: Blood and Steel* (1993). It starts as a typical direct-to-video thriller, with kung fu doctor Johnny (Don "The Dragon" Wilson) setting out to rescue his kidnapped fiancée, then takes a sharp left turn as he descends into the literal Los Angeles underground. There he runs a gamut of bizarrely

dressed gangs including the Shadow Warriors, the Garbage Gang, the Spacemen, and some Bad Girls. There's even a DJ (Charlie Ganis, a.k.a. filmmaker Charles T. Kanganis) who provides running commentary on the action!

Ring of Fire II's co-producer and fight choreographer Paul Maslak, who also helped come up with the film's story, recalls, "The influence of *The Warriors* was part of the original concept that Don 'The Dragon' and I discussed with the writers during the planning stages." It wasn't the only action classic they referenced: "*Blood and Steel* was the original working title for *Enter the Dragon*, so we put that in our title as a homage to Bruce Lee."

Aside from *Mad Max*, none of these films made nearly the impact of *The Warriors*, though—culturally or at the box office. Even after all the negative publicity, and losing some of its theaters as a result, the movie grossed over $22 million, giving Hill his first box-office hit. And as it turned out, he wasn't finished with the movie yet...

5 *The Warriors* Battles On

It turned out that Swan and the rest of the Warriors had a pretty bright future to fight for.

In February 1980, Paramount sent *The Warriors* back to theaters with a new ad campaign and tagline: "One year ago, one of the most talked-about movies of our time opened. If you missed it then, see it now." In many cities it was co-billed with *American Gigolo*, the studio's latest box-office hit, which features a memorable scene outside a theater showing *The Warriors*. (There's an inside joke here as well: The film's title on the exterior display has been crossed out with graffiti and tagged "VGV," a reference to Varrio Grande Vista from the competing gang film *Boulevard Nights*.) For most of the year, the film toured the nation's screens in regional release, sometimes as a single feature or doubled with another recent Paramount moneymaker, *Little Darlings*. One exception was Detroit, where it opened on December 5 with *Mandingo* as its co-feature in 12 theaters.

By then, *The Warriors* had already bopped its way into U.S. living rooms via three different routes: pay TV, home video, and Super 8mm film. Subscribers to the Movie Channel were the first to watch it at home in September 1980, but many more caught the film a month or so later when Home Box Office premiered it on Friday, October 31 at 9 p.m. Teens and preteens were just getting back from trick-or-treating at that time, hopped up on sugar and looking for something exciting to watch while sorting through their treats. A good amount of them tuned in to HBO that night for their first exposure to the movie, which became the talk of the schoolyard the following Monday.

For those with VCRs, October also marked the first time *The Warriors* became available on videocassette when Paramount Home Video issued the film on VHS and Beta. That same month, Select Film/Video released a feature-length Super 8 version on three 400-foot reels, one of seven Paramount films the mail-order company was selling in the format for $99.95 each (the others were *Barbarella*, *Black Sunday*, *Chinatown*, *Grease*, *Saturday Night Fever*, and *When Worlds Collide*).

This one shot from *American Gigolo* (1980) contains references to two different 1979 gang movies.

All of this helped expand the audience for *The Warriors* beyond midnight shows and drive-in/action-circuit subruns, where it had been languishing since Paramount's decision to pull it from first-run theaters. But what really etched its cult-film street cred in stone was its inclusion in Danny Peary's seminal book *Cult Movies*, published in November 1981. The first serious critical reassessment of the movie and the controversy surrounding it, Peary's insightful chapter on *The Warriors* described it as "a lively, well-made action film full of adventure and humor, no more violent than the film down the block, not inciteful, not deserving of the furor that it had caused."

Not only did *The Warriors'* extended shelf life encourage distributors to capitalize on its continued success into the early '80s (as discussed in Chapter Four), the biggest cash-in of all came from the producers of *The Warriors* themselves, Paramount and Lawrence Gordon, in August 1982. *The Renegades* was the two-hour TV pilot for a series about an interracial group of criminal gang members who are granted a reprieve when the police department recruits them for a new anti-crime task force designed to combat gang violence. A cocktail of equal parts *The Warriors* and *The Dirty Dozen* mixed with ABC's earlier hit *The Mod Squad* (with that show's producer, Aaron Spelling, credited as "creative consultant"), *The Renegades* was directed by Hill collaborator Roger Spottiswoode and features music by Barry DeVorzon, costumes by Bobbie Mannix, and stunts and second-unit direction by Craig Baxley. The gang members are named Eagle, Dragon, Dancer, and Gaucho, with Patrick Swayze heading the cast as the team's very Swan-like leader, Bandit.

The reviews were overwhelmingly negative, with at least one applauding the network's decision to pass on the series before the pilot had even aired. "This week's Good Taste in Television Award is presented to ABC for refusing to buy *The Renegades* for use as a new fall series," began Lee Winfrey's write-up for the Knight-Ridder News Service. "This rarely presented award has seldom been bestowed upon a more deserving winner. *The Renegades* could set TV back 20 years if its virus were allowed to spread."

Although the pilot was the number-six show for the week in the Nielsen ratings, ABC had a very good reason for not adding *The Renegades*

to its fall schedule: three months earlier, the trial of John Hinckley Jr. for the attempted assassination of President Ronald Reagan had reignited the fiery debate regarding movie and TV violence inspiring real-life violence. During the trial, it was argued that Hinckley's obsession with actress Jodie Foster and her role in *Taxi Driver* had driven him to commit a crime eerily similar to the one almost carried out by that film's protagonist, Travis Bickle (Robert De Niro).

This enraged media mogul Ted Turner, who appeared in a videotaped editorial in which he called for government action preventing Hollywood from making any more violent movies and stated that the Columbia Pictures executives responsible for the production and distribution of *Taxi Driver* "should be just as much on trial as John Hinckley himself." Turner also singled out *The Warriors*, claiming the latter was of "absolutely no redeeming social value," before telling his viewers, "If you are as concerned as I am, you should write your congressman and your senator right away and tell them that you want something done about these destructive motion pictures." The editorial aired 21 times over the Memorial Day weekend on Turner's own CNN and WTBS stations, and made national headlines.

To the brass at ABC, it may have seemed like Turner's editorial was also targeting them, albeit indirectly, since the network had shown *Taxi Driver* during prime time on *The ABC Sunday Night Movie* back in January 1979, where it was most likely viewed by Hinckley. Additionally, the network was in the process of preparing a TV-friendly version of *The Warriors*, another movie on Turner's hit list and already the source of in-house controversy: When the senior vice president of programming, Alfred Schneider, was first informed of the plan to broadcast the film in a 9-11 p.m. time slot, his response had been "Over my dead body!" Network editor Andre deSzekely, who specialized in preparing TV versions of controversial movies like *Taxi Driver*, *Shampoo*, and *Looking for Mr. Goodbar*, was given the job of readying *The Warriors* for prime time. After viewing it once, deSzekely described it as "an incentive to riot" and then went to work, making at least 128 deletions totaling six minutes of running time in order to conform the film to network standards. The editing process took almost a year to complete and involved the addition of five minutes of outtakes (detailed in Chapter Two), along with bringing back four of the lead actors to dub these added scenes and revoice new lines written by deSzekely to replace the film's myriad f-bombs and other expletives.

The announcement that ABC would be broadcasting *The Warriors* on *The ABC Friday Night Movie* on February 25, 1983 inspired outrage in Boston, where the stabbing death of Martin Yakubowicz four years earlier was still fresh in the minds of many citizens. *The Boston Globe* launched a campaign against both the movie and the local ABC affiliate, WCVB, publishing several articles in the days leading up to the scheduled airdate, most of them banged out by veteran newsman Jack Thomas. "It's true, as ABC says, that thanks to the editing, the television version is less violent, but only in the sense that a two-car accident is less violent than one involving three or four automobiles," he wrote in one editorial. "The problem with *The Warriors* is one that editing will not eliminate. *The Warriors* is violent by theme, and scissoring a scene here and there doesn't cleanse the whole." He ended the same piece by assuring his readers, "This is not a cry for censorship, but rather a complaint about bad taste on the part of ABC and the local affiliate, WCVB. In the end, *The Warriors* is an ugly, even dangerous movie that does not belong on prime-time television."

Cliff Curley, a vice president at WCVB-TV, screened the film and then called Thomas back to say, "I don't think it's unacceptable." The general manager, James Coppersmith, agreed. "Frankly, with all the things that have been on television, *The Warriors* is not going to have a destructive effect on our society," he told Thomas. "You're trying to 'issue-ize' this. You're trying to compare *The Warriors* to *Deep Throat*."

'Warrior' TV airing raises bitter specter

Edited 'Warriors' is still too violent

Meanwhile, the *Globe* sent another journalist, Joanne Ball, to get a statement from the family of the slain teenager, but since Mr. and Mrs. Yakubowicz were in the process of suing Paramount and the Saxon Theater Corp. of Boston for the wrongful death of their son, she had to settle for the older sister, Elaine Spileos. The interview was conducted in the office of the family's attorney, after which Ball went straight to her typewriter with exactly the type of quotes the *Globe* needed to further its agenda: "This movie could make someone do what happened four years ago. I really believe that"; "It's going to kick up emotion"; "I just think when you see a movie it can make individuals do things that they probably wouldn't have done if they hadn't seen it"; "I think [ABC] should have more social responsibility. They should look at things as what they would want their children to see"; "Put [*The Warriors*] on a shelf and let it collect cobwebs. I feel they've made enough money."

Naturally, certain activists of the day were also contacted for their expert opinions. "I have a feeling you could tell it was sweeps month just because films like *The Warriors* are being shown," cracked Peggy Charren of Action for Children's Television, while Dr. Thomas Radecki of the National Coalition on Television Violence—sticking closer to the *Globe*'s thesis—remarked, "There is no question about the damage this film causes. Evidence suggests the harm is far greater than three deaths. It changes the thinking and habits of probably tens of thousands of young men, causing them to become more aggressive and more likely to participate in gang and street-type crime. It glamorizes gangs and violence as a solution to problems."

(Did no one in Boston notice that *The Warriors* had just played without incident in two local theaters, the Somerville and Coolidge Corner, earlier in the same month?)

As a result of the *Globe*'s coverage, WCVB was flooded with over 15,000 telephone calls from viewers requesting that the station cancel the broadcast. Coppersmith finally yielded on Friday morning, airing a taped statement in which he said, "Channel 5 has always been sensitive to taste and the desires of the communities it serves. It has become clear to us that to carry the ABC broadcast of *The Warriors* tonight would be contrary to that philosophy. Therefore, we will not be carrying network programming during the 9 to 11 period this evening. We regret the publicity that has surrounded this event, but perhaps out of this controversy some good has arisen. It has given us the opportunity to communicate with our viewers, many of whom I have spoken with directly. While our programming decisions may not always be the correct ones, our actions today indicate that our attitude is always responsive, and we are grateful to our viewers for making their feelings known." WCVB filled the two-hour gap with the 1942 Katharine Hepburn movie *Woman of the Year*.

ABC reported that only one other affiliate, WJZ-TV in Baltimore, had also declined to broadcast *The Warriors* that night. However, TV critic Bill Collins of *The Philadelphia Inquirer* revealed five days later that WPVI Channel 6, ABC's affiliate in the City of Brotherly Love, had quietly replaced the broadcast of *The Warriors* with an even more problematic Paramount production, the sleazy rape-revenge thriller *Lipstick* (1976). In response to this bizarre programming decision, Collins wrote, "Channel 6 seems to have kept a movie of questionable merit off the air to show us one with no merit."

If there was one preemption ABC was unaware of, there were probably others, which might explain why the broadcast of *The Warriors* ended up being their lowest-rated program that week—number 65 on the Nielsen chart with an 11.4/18 rating share. It could also account for why the network started running the six unaired episodes of *The Renegades* in the same time slot a week later, which prompted Boston viewer Andrea Turner to write the following letter to the *Globe*: "On Friday, Feb. 25, Channel 5 decided not to broadcast the movie *The Warriors*, because of public complaints about its violence. I applauded the decision.

"A week later, on March 4, I was astounded and disturbed when I turned to Channel 5 at 9 p.m. And found a show similar to the one it had refused to air the previous week. The plot of this premiere, one-hour series, *The Renegades*, is that former gang leaders turn into undercover police officers.

"Whatever the cause, I saw two gangs in opposition to each other. Although their names were not the Warriors, these gangs wore leather jackets, masks, and carried chains. On the whole, the hour was filled with violence. The series almost certainly is a take-off on *The Warriors*.

"If *The Warriors* was so dangerous to our society that it was removed from prime time television by Channel 5, why then was *The Renegades* allowed to air? I really wish the television stations would get their priorities straight. Isn't one hour of street violence just as bad as two?" (During the month and a half the episodes aired, series regular Swayze could also be seen in theaters as one of the stars of the gang movie *The Outsiders*, based on S.E. Hinton's trailblazing young adult novel.)

Over the course of the next decade, analog formats like VHS gave way to improved digital presentations of movies in the home video market. The initial DVD of *The Warriors*, released by Paramount Home Video during the format's early days on January 16, 2001, was no-frills; this was the time when the Special Features listed on disc cases included "Interactive Menus," "Scene Selection," and "Theatrical Trailer." Five years later, however, Walter Hill decided to take advantage of the opportunity to reissue *The Warriors* as he had originally envisioned it.

On October 4, 2005, Paramount Home Entertainment, as it was now known, released *The Warriors* in an Ultimate Director's Cut (also issued on Blu-ray in 2007). With no changes to the live-action material, it adds a brief intro recounting the *Anabasis* legend via illustrated panels by Brian Murray, a noted comics and storyboard artist (*Chronicles of Riddick, Ready Player One, Solo: A Star Wars Story*), with narration by Hill himself. Similar Murray-drawn animated interstitials are dropped into the film at key transitional moments. Although Hill states in an introduction on the disc that he's not a fan of explanatory bonus features, believing "movies should speak for themselves," he and many of *The Warriors*' cast and creatives sat down for interviews used in a four-part documentary by disc-supplement master Laurent Bouzereau. The movie also received a new transfer that, like the doc, received positive notices from reviewers.

The critics weren't as taken with the illustrated intro and inserts, however. *The New York Times*' Dave Kehr wrote, "The effect is to emphasize the film's stylized approach and to underline its connections to classical literature—in other words, to back off from the violent immediacy that was blamed for a handful of gang incidents in theaters during the film's first engagement. It's an admirable humanistic gesture, but it does distract from the dark, ravishing beauty of Mr. Hill's hallucination of New York City in the down-and-out 70's." Many of the reactions matched that of Rob Watson of *The Philadelphia Inquirer*, who recommended, "For those of you who are really passionate about the film, hold on to your copy of the [original] DVD release... The changes end up being a little cheesy." DVDTalk.com's Ian Jane opined that the prologue "makes the comparison to the Greek myth on which the story is based about as subtle as a brick to the face," and that the new material in general "feels a little out of place and it makes this less the film we all know and love."

Jane also believed that the insert introducing the Baseball Furies ("Holy Shit!!!") flattens the dramatic impact of their reveal, and so did IGN.com's Peter Schorn. He wrote, "In the old version, we see shots of the Warriors reacting to something off-camera before we see what's disturbing them. Now, a couple of transition panels tell us we're changing locations and then we're shown the Furies...it does squander one of the most memorable moments."

The final knock was given by AVClub.com, which included the Ultimate Director's Cut in its survey of "13-plus movies weakened by directors' cuts." This article panned the animated bits as "a cutesy graphic context that disrupts the pacing and insults the audience by underlining the film's cartoonish hyperbole—as if people would otherwise mistake a gang in baseball gear and clown makeup for docu-realism."

Just a couple of weeks after the Director's Cut DVD hit, on October 17, 2005, a *Warriors* video game was released by Rockstar Games, best known for the notorious and enduring *Grand Theft Auto* series. Issued for the PlayStation 2 and Xbox, and later for PSP, PS3 and PS4, it was directed by Kevin Hoare and Greg Bick and produced by Rich Rasado. The action starts three months before that of the film, as players engage in assorted skirmishes and missions (from graffiti tagging to rumbles with rivals) before the Warriors are invited to the uptown meeting and the assassination storyline kicks in for the final sections. Members of the original cast returned to voice their characters, including Michael Beck (Swan), James Remar (Ajax), Deborah Van Valkenburgh (Mercy), Dorsey Wright (Cleon), David Harris (Cochise) and even Thomas G. Waites, despite his contentious history with *The Warriors*, as The Fox.

"I had to audition to play myself," Waites recalls. "My manager called me and said, 'You have an audition today for the video game of *The Warriors*.' I had done a lot of voice work in the '80s, selling Listerine or whatever the product was, so I considered it just another voice audition. I said, 'Well, what part am I reading for?' And they said, 'For yourself!' [*Laughs*] I said, 'You're kidding!' But I went in and I met the guy—a brilliant young kid, I can't remember his name—and he said, 'I just wanted to make sure

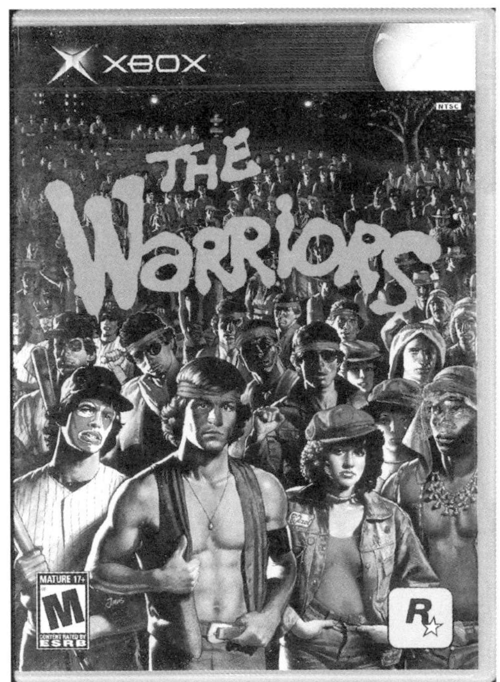

you haven't ruined your voice with cigarettes and alcohol, and that you still sound the same as you did when you did the movie.' And I said, 'That's fair.' So I worked, I think, two days on it, and it made tens of millions of dollars. Which I guess is why Rockstar is what it is. I didn't realize it at the time, but I think there was some vindication there for me, especially because the role of the Fox was a bit expanded.

"The video game has brought us a whole new crop of followers," he adds, "all these young kids who are like, 'I'd never even heard of the movie, dude, I just played the video game and loved it. And your character's my favorite one to play. And then I saw that it was a movie, and then I found out this and found out that...' It's quite wonderful. It's great to be part of the legacy, to be part of something that is still remembered."

Roger Hill is also heard in the game as Cyrus, though in 2006, he sued Rockstar and its owner, Take-Two Interactive Software, for using his voice and likeness without permission, after he passed on an offer to involve him in the game's production. Take-Two countered that they had a third-party license to replicate Hill as Cyrus.

The game additionally made use of DeVorzon's memorable score from the movie. Although Rockstar also offered customizable soundtracks online, the company considered DeVorzon's music crucial enough to pony up big bucks for it—though not at first. The composer was initially offered a token fee for his material, and turned it down. "The next time I heard from them," he relates in Tom Grieving's liner notes for La-La Land's CD release of the *Warriors* soundtrack, "they offered me $145,000. And that I took. I must admit that's what pleased me, the fact that they felt that music—which, gosh, by then should have been considered dated—was really important to that whole *Warriors* thing."

Critics responded positively to the game, which "didn't just retell the film—it added a huge amount of backstory to the characters and situations, and it was *good* backstory too," according to GameSpot.com's Alex Navarro. "On top of that, the gameplay served as some of the best beat-'em-up action you could find in the 3D era of gaming." AVClub.com's Scott Tobias was far more positive toward the game than his site was to the Ultimate Director's Cut, writing that Rockstar "plays note-perfect homage to the film while expanding its universe tenfold, turning *The Warriors* into the sort of vast gaming playground that has made the *GTA* series rise above its political notoriety...it opens up into reams of backstory and character detail that the movie couldn't possibly contain."

Another opportunity to relive the movie's adventures was offered by *The Warriors: Come Out to Play*, a cooperative strategy board game created by Prospero Hall and published by Funko in 2022. Players use mover pieces featuring the likenesses of Swan, the Fox, Mercy, Vermin, Cochise, Rembrandt, Snow, and Cowboy, traversing a board featuring a stylized relief map of Manhattan. The "Fight Phase" takes place in Van Cortlandt Park following Cyrus' murder, and the "City Phase" has players evading and battling rival gang members (represented by seven miniature figures) on the way to Coney Island.

Ajax is conspicuous by his absence as a playable character in *Come Out to Play*, and when a fan questioned this exclusion on the Boardgamegeek.com forums, Jesse Cromley of Funko replied, "It was a purposeful decision to not include Ajax. He is without question a character with dubious morals and yet, he is important to the story, serving as an antagonist to Swan, the main protagonist. Ajax exists to create tension and highlight the positive qualities in the other characters and exits the movie once this is achieved. Ajax's misgivings are his undoing; He never makes it to Coney Island in the movie and therefore is not a playable character." (A few responders then wondered why the latter disqualification didn't apply to the Fox, who exits the movie before Ajax.)

On top of that, 2005 saw the release of a series of 10-inch *Warriors* action figures by Mezco Toyz. The collection included Swan, Ajax, Cleon, Cochise, Luther, and three different Baseball Furies, each with a few weapons (aside from Ajax, whose fists are apparently enough). There were also a few limited-edition Furies produced, sold exclusively at Toywiz.com, plus another couple of Furies made specifically for San Diego Comic-Con. These stylized figures were followed the same year by a 9-inch Mezco series with more realistic appearances/proportions, consisting of Swan, Ajax, Cyrus, Sully (leader of the Orphans gang) and a pair of the ever-popular Furies. No longer manufactured, these figures sometimes fetch high prices on the collectors' market.

Since its theatrical release, *The Warriors* has often been compared to a comic book, so it was only a matter of time before one actually materialized. In January 2009, to commemorate the film's 30th anniversary, Dabel Brothers Publishing announced the release of *The Warriors* #1, the first issue in a five-part adaptation. Written by David Atchison and illustrated by Chris Dibari (penciller/inker), the series was slated to hit stores by month's end, with plans for spinoffs featuring several of the movie's iconic characters.

Even bigger news came shortly afterward at San Diego Comic-Con, when Dabel unveiled plans for a four-issue sequel, *The Warriors: Jailbreak*, with the first issue set for release in July 2009. The idea for a sequel had originated with pencil/ink artists Herb Apon and Todd Herman. "I had actually done some sample pages years before and went to Dark Horse to see if they could get the rights, but the timing was off," Apon explained to TFAW.com. "There was talk of a remake, and Paramount was not interested in a comic at that time."

Once Dabel Brothers secured the license, Apon and Herman began brainstorming story ideas for the characters, which were later handed over to writer Erik Henriksen. "Todd and Herb, since they're both ridiculously huge *Warriors* fans, already had some really killer ideas about where the story should go," Henriksen told the website, "and it was then that I got brought on to actually sit down and write the thing." Apon added, "Todd and I had tons of ideas, and I thought the book would have to be an anthology, short stories about the different gangs, but Erik somehow wove almost all of our ideas into one amazing storyline."

The main idea the two artists came up with centered on the fate of Ajax, who is last seen being dragged into the back of a police car. "Every time the film would end, the first thing I would think about was what would happen to Ajax?" said Herman. "Would he die in jail? Was he a Warrior anymore, or had he betrayed them? It just didn't make any sense to me that they would abandon him, and I felt very strongly that after the film ended, the Warriors' immediate focus would be on trying to help out their friend and comrade, if that were even possible."

With themes of brotherhood and camaraderie in mind, *The Warriors: Jailbreak* opens with a flashback to a fight between Swan and Ajax to determine who will be War Chief, second-in-command to Cleon. Swan wins the fight but makes a crucial mistake: He walks away, leaving Ajax on the ground. "You don't ever leave a Warrior behind," Cleon tells him. "Don't forget—we're *all* Warriors."

The story then jumps forward a few months after the events of the movie. Ajax is now being held at the Bronx House of Detention, a temporary facility used for instances when Rikers Island reaches capacity—like the night Cyrus was killed and the NYPD rounded up a large number of gang members at the conclave. In the jail with him are two members of the Gramercy Riffs, as well as a psychotic Baseball Fury who wants nothing more than to beat Ajax to death with a bat. The situation becomes more intense when two jail guards try to coerce Ajax into becoming an informant. They want him to reveal information on other gangs, which they plan to take to the commissioner's office. Instead of cooperating, Ajax defiantly mouths off about their mothers, earning himself a billy-club beatdown.

The rest of the Warriors learn that Ajax's days are numbered. Remembering Cleon's words about never leaving a Warrior behind, Swan starts to formulate a plan to break Ajax out. To pull it off, he leads the Warriors into an uneasy alliance with the Gramercy Riffs, since two of their own are being held in the same jail.

In one of the subplots, Mercy has parted ways with Swan and is now living as a kept woman, supported by a married office worker who provides her with an apartment. "We took away Swan and Mercy's happy ending," Herman told TFAW.com. "We didn't want to make it quite so easy for them to just walk into the sunset like they did at the end of the film." Rembrandt draws a sketch of Mercy at one point and offers it to Swan, who declines it and says, "Nice try, Rembrandt, but you forgot to draw the dollar signs in her eyes."

As for Rembrandt, he's taking painting lessons in Manhattan but finding his artistic aspirations are increasingly in conflict with his responsibilities to the gang. On the subway ride to the Bronx to bust Ajax out of jail, his painting teacher sees him with the other Warriors and implores him to leave gang life behind ("You aren't the only kid who's ever wanted to belong."). In another scene, Rembrandt scolds a new member for questioning Swan's loyalty to Ajax ("It doesn't matter if Swan likes him or not, D-Train. Ajax is a *Warrior*."). "I think other than breaking Ajax out of jail, this story is about Rembrandt defining to himself what it means to be a Warrior," Herman said. Although *The Warriors: Jailbreak* ends with hints of more to come regarding the Mercy and Rembrandt subplots, Dabel Brothers never published additional Warriors stories.

And like pretty much every other '70s cult favorite, *The Warriors* was talked up for a remake in the 2000s. Hill told TheFader.com's Eric Ducker, "[Producer] Larry Gordon and I laughed about that they've probably got as much money in [reboot] scripts now as it probably took us to make the movie." The filmmaker attached for a number of years was Tony Scott, who planned to set the story in Los Angeles and stage martial-arts brawls in the style of Asian action cinema between the Warriors and their enemies, who in his vision would number in the thousands. He explained another difference to Rotten Tomatoes' Joe Utichi: "New York is vertical, all skyscrapers, and Los Angeles is horizontal." For this more sprawling story, "I've been meeting the various gangs as part of the research... I've met them all, Crips, Bloods, The 18th Street Gang, The Vietnamese and so on. They all love *The Warriors*. So it was, 'yeah, fuck yeah we'll be in that!' "

One of his ambitions wound up with tragic echoes three years later. Scott said, "I'm hoping to get a hundred thousand real gang-members standing on the Vincent Thomas Bridge for one shot." On August 19, 2012, Scott jumped to his death from that landmark span into Los Angeles Harbor.

In 2016, it was once again announced that *The Warriors* would be rebooted, this time as a one-hour series for Paramount TV and Hulu, with Gordon serving as executive producer. Marvel-movie masters Joe and Anthony Russo (*Captain America: The Winter Soldier* and *Civil War*; *The Avengers: Infinity War* and *Endgame*) were attached to direct the pilot, with Frank Baldwin scripting the show. The project was announced as having moved to Netflix in 2018, but no further progress was made.

In between discussions about these onscreen second chapters, an actual reunion of *The Warriors'* original cast took place on August 2, 2006 at a screening of the movie in Coney Island. It was the first stop on the Netflix Rolling Roadshow, a touring film festival that screened 10 classic movies throughout the U.S., most in key locations where they were filmed. Co-sponsored by the Alamo Drafthouse Cinema chain and hosted by Grammy-winning singer-songwriter Lisa Loeb, the Rolling Roadshow also brought cast members and filmmakers to some of the screenings, and the special guests who showed up for *The Warriors* in Coney Island were Michael Beck, Deborah Van Valkenburgh, Dorsey Wright, David Harris, and Terry Michos. Hundreds of fans lined up to meet them and get their autographs, and a subway scavenger hunt was held before the screening. Artist Bobby Dixon of Kollective Fusion designed a 23x32 limited-edition poster that references more activities that may have been planned for the event ("*recreate the route of the Warriors*," "*compete in the Warriors subway rally*," "*meet in gang attire at noon on August 2 at the site of the conclave*").

A similar event occurred on September 13, 2015 at Coney Island's Surf Pavilion. The "Last Subway Ride Reunion" was organized by wrestler-turned-actor Eric Nyenhuis, and brought Beck, Waites, Wright, Harris, and Michos together to take the Q train down to Coney, recreating their ride from the film. Once there, they were joined by numerous other co-stars and stuntmen, plus throngs of fans (including kids), many of them dressed or tattooed after *Warriors* characters. "I just love being here with all the fans," Beck told *Rolling Stone* at the scene. "I see kids coming here, eight years old, and I go 'How do you even know about this movie?' I found out something today. One of the stunt guys who played one of the Furies, he came up to me and told me, 'Thirty-seven years ago, you broke three of my ribs with a baseball bat.' I told him I was sorry. I didn't mean to."

Revelations of unknown injuries aside, it was a joyous occasion, a celebration of a movie that has lived on in the hearts and minds of countless fans for four decades...but even this event was touched by a spot of controversy. Shortly before it took place, photographer Joe Russo (no relation to the aforementioned director) posted on Facebook that the reunion was his idea, that he had partnered with Nyenhuis, and that the latter's "shady actions and lack of business ethics" had led him to depart during the planning stages. Nyenhuis fired back that Russo had reneged on an agreement to put up half of the money, and as a result was asked to step away from it.

In the years since the Last Subway Ride, *Warriors* cast members have appeared at numerous comic/cult/horror conventions and other events to do signings, photo ops, and panel discussions related to the movie. For example, Harris and Michos were special guests at the Mahoning Drive-In theater in August 2022 for a Walter Hill triple feature of *The Warriors*, *Hard Times*, and *The Driver*. Chiller Theatre in New Jersey is one of the largest and most popular fan conventions on the circuit, and its April 2024 show assembled the biggest Warriors reunion yet with Beck, Harris, Michos, Tyler, Waites, and Wright as special guests, plus Craig Baxley, Fernando Castillo, Eddie Earl Hatch, Bobbie Mannix, Apache Ramos, Rob Ryder, Konrad Sheehan, Deborah Van Valkenburgh, and Joel Weiss also in attendance. The highlight of the April 2025 Chiller was a reunion of the Lizzies, featuring Iris Alahanti, Dee Dee Benrey, Doran Clark, Kate Klugman, Lisa Maurer, and Wanda Velez. With references to *The Warriors* cropping up in video games, movies, TV shows and commercials, hip-hop, music videos, and all sorts of Internet memes and skits, the film's supporters now

number far more than just those who discovered it through Rockstar Games or fell in love with it decades ago, while in their youth.

One of those latter fans was Lin-Manuel Miranda, award-winning creator of the hit Broadway musicals *In the Heights* (2008) and *Hamilton* (2015), who was first exposed to *The Warriors* at 4 years of age when the older brother of one of his friends popped it into a VCR while the youngsters were in the room. The film made a strong impression on Miranda, who re-watched it countless times in the ensuing years, especially during summer vacations in Puerto Rico, where his grandfather owned a video rental shop that stocked the Paramount videotape. Shortly after *In the Heights* won the Tony Award for Best Musical, Miranda received an e-mail from a college friend who had just started working for Gordon and proposed the idea of turning the cult favorite into a stage musical. Miranda sent back a response listing all the reasons why it couldn't be done, but filed the idea away in his mind.

Seven years later, after finishing his Broadway run in *Hamilton*, Miranda found himself again thinking about *The Warriors* as a musical, only this time approaching the idea from a different angle: gender-flipping the Warriors into an all-female gang. His inspiration? The GamerGate controversy from a couple of years earlier, which he described to *The New York Times'* Michael Paulson as "these extremely online dudes [who] were doxxing women just for the cruelty and the chaos of it." To Miranda, the behavior of these misogynistic men was similar to Luther shooting Cyrus and then blaming the Warriors for the murder of the revered gang leader. "And suddenly the Warriors' lives are ruined, and they have to fight their way home with every dude in the city trying to kill them," he told the *Times*. "And I think that's when my brain made the gender flip."

To co-write the script with him, he approached Obie Award-winning actress and Pulitzer Prize-nominated playwright Eisa Davis. Despite being unfamiliar with the story, Davis found the premise intriguing and Miranda's enthusiasm for it infectious, even if the original movie left her cold on first impression. "With all due respect, the film has a lot of misogyny and a lot of homophobia, and that went over in 1979 for some people, but I can't brook that," she told *The New York Times*. For more thematic inspiration, Davis leaned on her knowledge of a real-life event known as the Hoe Avenue peace meeting, which occurred in 1971 when rival gangs met at the Madison Square Boys Club in the Bronx to set their differences aside and sign a peace treaty. Even though it ushered in a new era of block parties, rapping, breakdancing, and graffiti art, this historical turning point came with its own set of baggage. "The women who were at that peace meeting were made to sit in the back, and the gangs that were all femme were not even allowed to come into that meeting. So in some ways, I feel like this is a vindication for them." The gender-flipping aspect of their *Warriors*, she told NPR's *Morning Edition*, enabled them to leave those outdated views in the past while giving the story a more contemporary feel.

The news that Miranda was writing a musical version of *The Warriors* for Broadway was first reported by the *New York Post* on August 3, 2023. A full year later, Miranda and Davis released a joint statement in which they clarified that their musical *Warriors* was not a stage production but a concept album, to be released by Atlantic Records on October 18, 2024. "We've spent the past three years musicalizing the Warriors' journey home, from the South Bronx to Coney Island," they said. "Along the way we've gotten to work with a lot of our favorite artists, and we'll be announcing their roles on the album in the weeks ahead."

On the day *Warriors* hit the streets, Miranda told NPR's *Morning Edition* that he and Davis had been inspired by their favorite concept albums from the '70s, like *Tommy* by The Who, *The Lamb Lies Down on Broadway* by Genesis, and *Jesus Christ Superstar*, "where you would sit on your living room floor and read the liner notes to your vinyl." Because of this, Atlantic released *Warriors* as a two-LP set with the full libretti printed in two booklets. The album was also made available as a two-CD set with booklets.

The first track is an explosive earworm called "Survive the Night," featuring Jamaican dancehall singer Shenseea as DJ Lynne Pen and a half-dozen iconic New York hip-hop stars representing the boroughs they come from: Chris Rivers as The Bronx, Nas as Queens, Cam'ron as Manhattan, RZA and Ghostface Killah as Staten Island, and Busta Rhymes as Brooklyn.

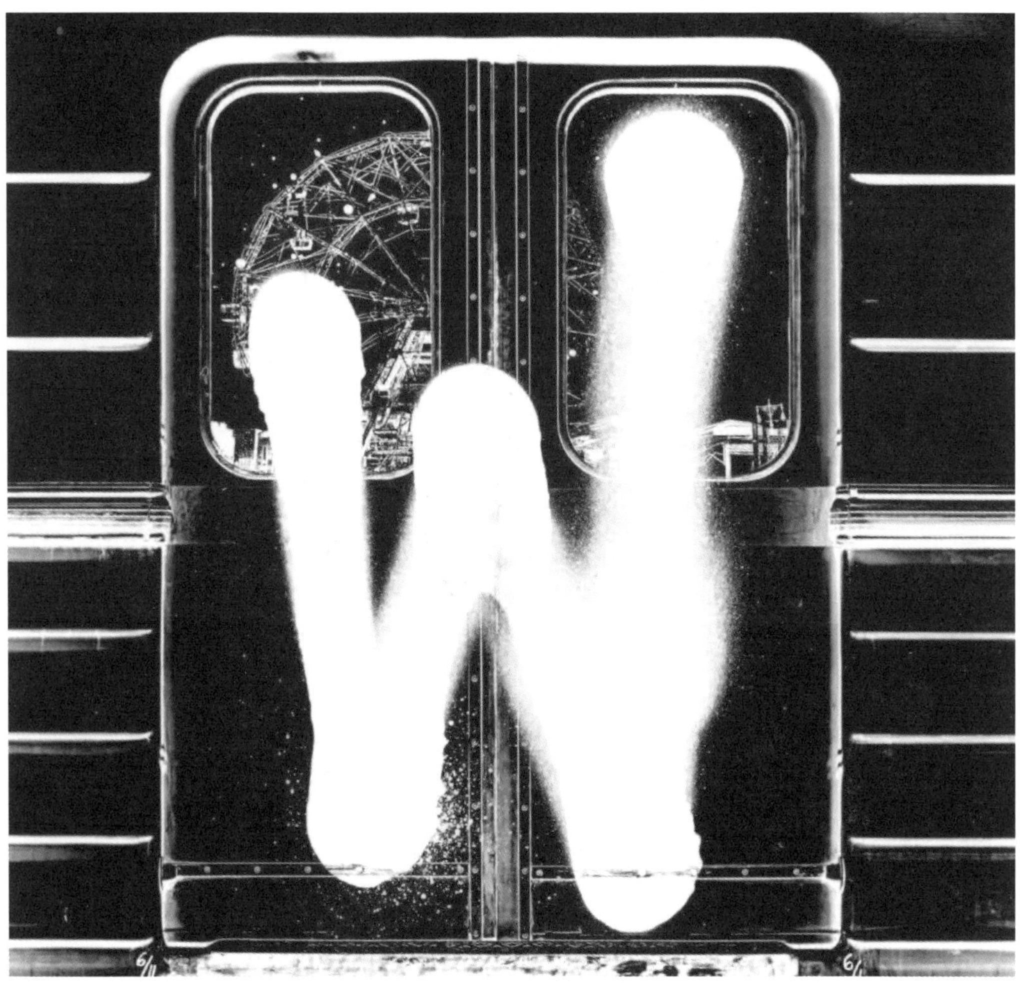

Other celebrity guests include Ms. Lauryn Hill as Cyrus; Colman Domingo as her second-in-command, Masai; Marc Anthony, Flaco Navaja, and Luis Figueroa as the Turnbull A.C.'s (reimagined as a Nuyorican crew that performs a catchy salsa number called "Leave the Bronx Alive"); David Patrick Kelly as one of the subway cops; and, in the most inspired bit of casting, James Remar as the police decoy who busts Ajax in Riverside Park.

The second track, "Roll Call," introduces the seven delegates from the Warriors—Cochise, Cowgirl, Fox, Cleon, Ajax, Rembrandt, and Swan (no Vermin or Snowball here)—in the form of a roll call that gets repeated several times during the night as the members get separated from one another or killed off. Australian indie rocker Kim Dracula plays Luther as a shrieking heavy-metal supervillain. One intriguing revision to the story is having the Gramercy Riffs take Cleon hostage rather than karate-chopping him to death. Other fun changes are the results of gender fluidity, like the Lizzies of the original becoming a boy band called the Bizzies, or the Mercy character remaining a woman and having a same-sex romance with Swan.

In an interview with Sarah Bahr published in *The New York Times* in December 2024, Miranda revealed that there just might be a Broadway musical of *Warriors* in the works after all. "We released the album for *Warriors* in October, and people really like it," he explained, "but because we're such a visual culture, everyone said to me and Eisa, 'OK, when can we see it?' So I think at the top of the year, Eisa and I will just start having conversations about how to adapt that to the stage."

And as a footnote to all these official/endorsed follow-ups and spinoffs, mention should be made of RevolutionWorks Ltd.'s unofficial sequel *Warriors: AlamoCity*. Essentially a shot-on-video (with Canon SD cameras) fan flick relocating the action to San Antonio, TX, it began shooting in 2009 under directors Frank Ramirez and Lauren Garrison and premiered at San Antonio's Josephine Theater on October 22, 2010. The story focuses on a Lone Star State chapter of the Warriors facing the threat of a new, especially violent gang called "the Unknown Clique," who have assaulted an innocent teenager.

An on-line announcement of *AlamoCity* boasted, "The film incorporates an improvised script, zero-dollar budget [and] day-of location shooting." So when it made its way to Amazon Prime (where its page is now inactive, no doubt due to cease-and-desists), it's not surprising that customer reviews included such comments as "This is NOT a movie. It is unwatchable garbage," "Any way to rate this movie with negative stars?", "This has to be one of the worst movies ever," and "This is not even grade school level filmmaking."

The original *Warriors* also received plenty of pans upon its first release, of course. But somehow, we don't see *AlamoCity* ascending to the iconic status that the first film has achieved, and that it will no doubt continue to enjoy as new generations discover it.

Acknowledgments

Thanks to Frankie Balboa @TimesSqKungFU, Elwaldo Baptiste, Virgil F. Cardamone, David Copeland, Michael Garfield Levine, Bobbie Mannix, Paul Maslak, Terry Michos, Apache Ramos, Edwin Samuelson, Francesco Simeoni, David Sosna, Thomas G. Waites, Joel Weiss, David Wilentz and William S. Wilson.

Special thanks to Rob Ryder, who took time from writing his own book to help us out with ours (Check out *Purple Fury: Rumbling with the Warriors*—it's great!).

Image Credits

Paramount Television / Cinematic / Alamy—33
Paramount / TCD / Prod.DB / Alamy—34, 35, 37-39, 42, 44-46, 48 (top), 61, 67, 71, 72, 82, 84, 87, 97, 104, 106
Paramount / Moviestore Collection Ltd. / Alamy—36, 102
Paramount / Collection Christophel / Alamy—41, 49, 63, 80, 93
Paramount / Photo 12 / Alamy—48 (bottom), 73
Paramount / A&M Records / Vinyl / Alamy—76
Cannon Group / Cinematic / Alamy—53
Paramount / Cinematic / Alamy—54
Colaimages / Alamy—59
Paramount / Everett Collection, Inc. / Alamy—110

Additional images and newspaper clippings are from the collections of Michael Gingold and Chris Poggiali.

Classics Illustrated cover (page 20) is © Classic Comic Store (Thorpe & Porter, 1976 English translation of *Illustrerade Klassiker* #170, Sweden, 1964).

Special thanks: Penguin (page 12), Holt Rinehart Winston (22), William Morrow (27), Dell (28-left), Italian Readers' Club (28-right), Warner Bros. (125), Cinematic Releasing (128), Toei Company (129-130), Independent-International Pictures (131), Lauren Films (132), Paramount (136), Paramount Home Video (143), Rockstar Games (145), Funko Games (147), Mezco Toyz (148), Dynamite Entertainment (149), The Mahoning Drive-In (153), and Atlantic Records (156).

Source Notes

Auster, Al and Georgakas, Dan, "*The Warriors*: An Interview with Sol Yurick," *Cineaste*, Spring 1979

Austin, Chuck, "Andy Laszlo, ASC: Night Cinematography for 'The Warriors,'" *Filmmaker Monthly*, January 1979

Bahr, Sarah, "Lin-Manuel Miranda on 'Mufasa' and the Secret to a Disney Hit," *The New York Times*, December 22, 2024

Ball, Joanne, "'Warrior' TV Airing Raises Bitter Specter," *The Boston Globe*, February 25, 1983

Baltake, Joe, "'Warriors' Would Rather Fight Than Face Up," *Philadelphia Daily News*, February 12, 1979

Beck, Marilyn, "Unforeseen violence haunts teen-gang movie producers," *The Journal News*, February 27, 1979

Bell, Arthur, "Wild in the Aisles," *Village Voice*, March 5, 1979

Blais, Madeleine, "What Price a Dream," *The Washington Post*, May 6, 1979

Blank, Ed, "'Warriors' Gangs Up On Unwary Audience," *Pittsburgh Press*, February 12, 1979

Canby, Vincent, "When a Tame Film Inspires Violence," *The New York Times*, March 4, 1979

Carducci, Mark Patrick, "On Location: *The Warriors*," *Millimeter*, December 1978

Clark, Ted and Borger, Lenny, "'Warriors' Faces X (Porn) Rating In France; Street Rowdy Fears; Limits May Kill Release There," *Variety*, July 11, 1979

Cocchi, John, "Youthful Cast of Para's 'Warriors' Will Not Be Unknowns Much Longer," *Boxoffice*, March 5, 1979

Collins, Bill, "'M*A*S*H' Carryover Audience Brings Top Rating to 'Live at 11,'" *The Philadelphia Inquirer*, March 2, 1983

Connolly, Bill, "Steve James Interview," *M.A.M.A. Martial Arts Movie Associates* #3, Spring 1986

Connor, Jackson, "Remember 'The Warriors,'" *Village Voice*, September 9, 2015

Dale, Bob, "This 'Family' Unwholesome," *The San Antonio Express and News*, September 26, 1965

Ducker, Eric, "New York Mythology," *TheFader.com*, October 3, 2005

Ebert, Roger, *Boulevard Nights* review, *Chicago Sun-Times*, May 7, 1979

Ebert, Roger, *The Warriors* review, *Chicago Sun-Times*, February 13, 1979

Ebert, Roger, "Why do so many people groove to 'The Warriors'?," *Detroit Free Press*, February 26, 1979 (sourced from *Chicago Sun-Times*)

Farrara, Frank, "Our Reviewers Report: Youth Gangs," *Daily Independent Journal*, August 21, 1965

Fleming, Mike Jr., "Tony Danza Takes Puncher's Chance With 'Honeymoon in Vegas': The Long Road That Got Him to Broadway," *Deadline.com*, January 14, 2015

Frakes, James R., "Hell on Turf," *The New York Times*, January 29, 1967

Gallick, Joe, "Warriors," *Daily News*, March 4, 1979

Grieving, Tom, "Rhythm & Attitude," *The Warriors* CD liner notes, La-La Land Records, 2013

"An Evening With *The Warriors*' David Harris," *The Five Count*, KMSU radio, April 12. 2014

Harris, Mary, "The fuss about 'Warriors' evades her; it's just boring," *Times Herald*, March 24, 1979

Hatch, Robert, "Yuricks Way," *The Nation*, November 22, 1965

Hemphill, Jim, "His Role as an Extra on 'The Warriors' Got Robert Townsend Thinking Like a Director," *IndieWire*, March 2, 2023

Hill, Walter, introduction on *The Warriors* Ultimate Director's Cut DVD, Paramount Home Entertainment, 2005

David Holden interview, *The Warriors Movie Site*, undated

Hoyt, Charles Alva, "Gamut of First Novels," *The Courier-Journal*, September 12, 1965

Hyman, Dan, "The Unexpected Score," *Village Voice*, September 9, 2015

Irving, Christopher, *Larry Hama: Conversations*, University Press of Mississippi, 2019

Jane, Ian, *The Warriors*: Ultimate Director's Cut DVD review, *DVDTalk.com*, October 3, 2005

Jones, Gareth, Tom McKitterick interview, *The Warriors Movie Site*, undated

Kael, Pauline, "The Current Cinema: Rumbling," *The New Yorker*, March 5, 1979

Kehr, Dave, *The Warriors*: Ultimate Director's Cut DVD review, *The New York Times*, October 11, 2005

Kipp, Jeremiah, "The Quiet Cool of a Gypsy Actor: An Interview with James Remar," *Shock Cinema* #19, Fall/Winter 2001

Laszlo, Andrew, *Every Frame a Rembrandt: Art and Practice of Cinematography*, Focal Press, 2000

Leahy, Jack and Mulligan, Arthur, "Dirty dozen see 'Warriors' & ape film in IND," *Daily News*, February 17, 1979

Lushbough, Juliet Dee, "Media Accountability for Real-Life Violence: A Case of Negligence or Free Speech?," *Journal of Communication*, June 1987

Markowitz, Robert, "Visual History with Walter Hill," *DGA.org*, undated

Maslin, Janet, "Movie: 'Warriors' Creates Visual Style That Is Stark," *The New York Times*, February 10, 1979

Meyer, Jeff, "Interview with the Creators of *Warriors: Jailbreak*," *GoCollect.com*, July 15, 2009, Interview by Elisabeth@TFAW.com

Meyers, Laura Scott, "The Bookshelf," *El Paso Herald-Post*, September 11, 1965

Navarro, Alex, *The Warriors* video game review, *GameSpot.com*, February 13, 2007

No author credited, "AIP Buys Movie, Book Rights for 1970 Movie Schedule," *Reno Evening Gazette*, July 12, 1969

No author credited, "Catholics Condemn, Kael Commends Par's 'Warriors,'" *Variety*, March 7, 1979

No author credited, "Film about gangs tied to 2 deaths, subway rampage," *Detroit Free Press*, February 19, 1979 (sourced from Associated Press)

No author credited, "Par Tries to Take Heat Off 'Warriors,'" *Variety*, February 21, 1979

No author credited, "Par, USA Cinemas Seek Dismissal Of A Lawsuit Centered On 'Warriors,'" *Variety*, August 12, 1987

No author credited, "Small Cities Eye 'Warriors' Wryly," *Variety*, March 28, 1979

No author credited, "The unkindest cut: 13-plus movies weakened by directors' cuts," *AVClub.com*, June 5, 2012

No author credited, "Watch 'The Warriors' Recreate Their Last Subway Ride Home," *RollingStone.com*, September 23, 2015

No author credited, "Walter Hill Disowns 'Warriors,' Goldman Defends Necessary Cuts," *Variety*, October 1, 1980

No author credited, "'Warriors' Exploitation Pays Off," *Boxoffice*, February 26, 1979

No author credited, "'Warriors' Fallout Is Minimal in East," *Boxoffice*, March 5, 1979

Paulson, Michael, "'The Warriors' Hooked Lin-Manuel Miranda at 4. Now Comes the Album," *The New York Times*, October 18, 2024

Peary, Danny, *Cult Movies*, Delta, 1981

"Poll," *The Warriors* review, *Variety*, February 14, 1979

Pryce-Jones, Alan, "Lethal Tale of Gangs," *The Philadelphia Inquirer*, September 19, 1965

Ramirez, Frank, *Warriors: AlamoCity* Movie Trailer, *FilmProposals.com*, undated

Riley, Mary Ann, "Iowa Bookshelf: New Books in Review," *Carroll Daily Times Herald*, August 28, 1965

Rosensohn, Sam, "'Warriors' movie triggers violence in theaters here," *New York Post*, February 16, 1979

Sarris, Andrew, *The Warriors* review, *Village Voice*, March 12, 1979

Schaumberg, Ron, "Violence Surrounding 'The Warriors' Is Apparently Unrelated to Film, Say Police and Circuit Officials," *Boxoffice*, date unknown

Schorn, Peter, *The Warriors*: Ultimate Director's Cut DVD review, *IGN.com*, October 19, 2005

Schreger, Charles, "Keeping an Eye on 'Warriors,'" *Los Angeles Times*, February 26, 1979

Seidenberg, Carol, "Young City Toughs Follow Course of *Odyssey*," *The Journal-News*, September 2, 1965

Shippy, Dick, "Gang rumble? How about stumble," *Akron Beacon-Journal*, February 20, 1979

Silverman, Stephen M., "A gang movie grows in B'klyn," *New York Post*, 14 July 1978

Siskel, Gene, "The gang cliches are all here in a weak 'Warriors,'" *Chicago Tribune*, February 13, 1979

Sorensen, Bob, "Book News: No Mommy's Boys or Daddy's Boys," *Minneapolis Tribune*, November 28, 1965

Talbot, Paul, "Swan Song: An Interview with Actor Michael Beck," *Shock Cinema* #41, 2011

Thomas, Jack, "Ch. 5 Cancels 'Warriors' Film," *The Boston Globe*, February 26, 1983

Thomas, Jack, "Edited 'Warriors' Is Still Too Violent," *The Boston Globe*, February 25, 1983

Thomas, Jack, "'Warriors' Stirs a TV Controversy," *The Boston Globe*, February 23, 1983

Tobias, Scott, *The Warriors* video game review, *AVClub.com*, November 2, 2005

Turner, Andrea, "One Hour of TV Violence as Bad as Two," letter to the editor, *The Boston Globe*, March 15, 1983

UPI News Service, "Ted Turner Stands Firm on Disputed TV Editorial," June 9, 1982

Utichi, Joe, "Exclusive: Tony Scott Talks *Warriors*," *Rottentomatoes.com*, June 2, 2009

Vanasco, Jennifer, "Lin-Manuel Miranda's New Musical Is Based on a Cult Movie—and Is for Your Ears Only," NPR's *Morning Edition*, October 18, 2024

The Warriors production notes, Paramount Pictures, 1979

Warriors: AlamoCity Amazon Prime page

"*The Warriors*: Battleground," *The Warriors* Ultimate Director's Cut DVD, Paramount Home Entertainment, 2005

"*The Warriors*: The Beginning," *The Warriors* Ultimate Director's Cut DVD, Paramount Home Entertainment, 2005

"*The Warriors*: The Phenomenon," *The Warriors* Ultimate Director's Cut DVD, Paramount Home Entertainment, 2005

"*The Warriors*: The Way Home," *The Warriors* Ultimate Director's Cut DVD, Paramount Home Entertainment, 2005

Watson, Rob, "Director diminishes 'The Warriors,'" *The Philadelphia Inquirer*, October 7, 2005

William V. Yakubowicz vs. Paramount Pictures Corporation & another, December 8, 1988-April 18, 1989

Winfrey, Lee, *The Renegades* review, Knight-Ridder News Service, August 11, 1982

Yurick, Sol, "How I Came to Write *The Warriors* and What Happened After," *The Warriors*, New York: Grove Press, 2003

About the Authors

MICHAEL GINGOLD began writing about movies as a teenager, editing and publishing the fanzine *Scareaphanalia*. He has been a writer and editor for *Fangoria* magazine since 1988 and its website since 2000. He is also a regular contributor to *Rue Morgue* magazine and Rue-morgue.com, *Delirium* magazine, and Inverse.com, and has written for *Birth.Movies.Death* and *Time Out New York* in print and on-line, *Scream* magazine, and IndieWire.com. Michael is the author of the *Ad Nauseam* and *Ad Astra* books (1984 Publishing), the novelization of *Nightmare* (Severin), and *The FrightFest Guide to Monster Movies* (FAB Press). He has directed documentaries and other bonus features, written liner notes, and taken part in audio commentaries for Blu-ray releases from Arrow Video, Severin Films, Vinegar Syndrome, Synapse Films, Shout! Factory, Blue Underground, Mondo Macabro and others, including the award-winning doc *Twisted Tale: The Unmaking of "Spookies"* for Vinegar Syndrome.

CHRIS POGGIALI is the co-author (with Grady Hendrix) of *These Fists Break Bricks: How Kung Fu Movies Swept America and Changed the World* (Running Press, 2025). He is a librarian, film historian and Rondo-nominated writer who edited the fanzine *Temple of Schlock* from 1987-1991, and brought it back as a blog in 2008. He has written for Turner Classic Movies, *Cinema Retro*, *Fangoria*, *Rue Morgue*, *HorrorHound*, *Shock Cinema*, *Filmfax*, *The Phantom of the Movies' Videoscope*, *Delirium*, *Deep Red*, *Eastern Heroes*, and other magazines and websites. His essays, commentaries and additional special features have appeared on DVD/Blu-ray releases from Kino Lorber, Shout! Factory, Vinegar Syndrome, Arrow Films, Severin Films, Synapse Films, 88 Films, Eureka Entertainment, Mondo Macabro, Something Weird Video, and other companies.

Park

Jerome Av

Mosholu Pky
Jerome Av

Bedford Pk Blvd-200 St
Jerome Av

Kingsbridge Rd
Jerome Av

Fordham Rd
Jerome Av

183 St
Jerome Av

Burnside Av
New York Univ
Jerome Av

176 St
Jerome Av

Mt Eden Av
Jerome Av

170 St
Jerome Av

167 St
River Av

IND
CC
D

IRT

205 St
Bainbridge Av

IND

CC

Bedford Pk Blvd
Concourse

Kingsbridge Rd
Concourse

Fordham Rd
Concourse

182-183 St
Concourse

Tremont Av
Concourse

174-175 St
Concourse

170 St
Concourse

167 St
Concourse

161 St-River Av
Yankee Stadium

149 St
Grand
Concourse

IRT

Gun Hill Rd
Webster Av

204 St
Webster Av

Bedford Pk
Blvd-200 St
Webster Av

Fordham Rd
3 Av

183 St
3 Av

Bronx
Park

180 St
3 Av

E Tremont Av-177
3 Av

174 St
3 Av

Claremont
Pky-3 Av

169 St
3 Av

166 St
3 Av

161 St
3 Av

156 St
3 Av

149 St
3 Av